▶ The Foreign Aid Regime

DOI: 10.1057/9781137505903.0001

Other Palgrave Pivot titles

C. J. T. Talar and Lawrence F. Barmann (editors): **Roman Catholic Modernists Confront the Great War**

Bernard Kelly: **Military Internees, Prisoners of War and the Irish State during the Second World War**

James Raven: **Lost Mansions: Essays on the Destruction of the Country House**

Luigino Bruni: **A Lexicon of Social Well-Being**

Michael Byron: **Submission and Subjection in Leviathan: Good Subjects in the Hobbesian Commonwealth**

Andrew Szanajda: **The Allies and the German Problem, 1941–1949: From Cooperation to Alternative Settlement**

Joseph E. Stiglitz and Refet S. Gürkaynak: **Taming Capital Flows: Capital Account Management in an Era of Globalization**

Steffen Mau: **Inequality, Marketization and the Majority Class: Why Did the European Middle Classes Accept Neo-Liberalism?**

Amelia Lambelet and Raphael Berthele: **Age and Foreign Language Learning in School**

Justin Robertson: **Localizing Global Finance: The Rise of Western-Style Private Equity in China**

Isabel Dulfano: **Indigenous Feminist Narratives: I/We: Wo(men) of an(Other) Way**

Stefan Lund: **School Choice, Ethnic Divisions, and Symbolic Boundaries**

Daniel Wirls: **The Federalist Papers and Institutional Power: In American Political Development**

Marcus Morgan and Patrick Baert: **Conflict in the Academy: A Study in the Sociology of Intellectuals**

Robyn Henderson and Karen Noble: **Professional Learning, Induction and Critical Reflection: Building Workforce Capacity in Education**

Graeme Kirkpatrick: **The Formation of Gaming Culture: UK Gaming Magazines, 1981–1995**

Candice C. Carter: **Social Education for Peace: Foundations, Teaching, and Curriculum for Visionary Learning**

Dilip K. Das: **An Enquiry into the Asian Growth Model**

Jan Pakulski and Bruce Tranter: **The Decline of Political Leadership in Australia? Changing Recruitment and Careers of Federal Politicians**

Christopher W. Hughes: **Japan's Foreign and Security Policy under the 'Abe Doctrine': New Dynamism or New Dead End?**

DOI: 10.1057/9781137505903.0001

palgrave▸pivot

The Foreign Aid Regime: Gift-Giving, States and Global Dis/Order

▶

Annalisa Furia

Research Fellow, University of Bologna, Italy

palgrave
macmillan

DOI: 10.1057/9781137505903.0001

First published 2015 by
PALGRAVE MACMILLAN

Palgrave Macmillan in the UK is an imprint of Macmillan Publishers Limited, registered in England, company number 785998, of Houndmills, Basingstoke, Hampshire RG21 6XS.

Palgrave Macmillan in the US is a division of St Martin's Press LLC, 175 Fifth Avenue, New York, NY 10010.

Palgrave Macmillan is the global academic imprint of the above companies and has companies and representatives throughout the world.

Palgrave® and Macmillan® are registered trademarks in the United States, the United Kingdom, Europe and other countries.

ISBN: 978-1-137-50591-0 EPUB
ISBN: 978-1-137-50590-3 PDF
ISBN: 978-1-137-50589-7 Hardback

A catalogue record for this book is available from the British Library.

A catalog record for this book is available from the Library of Congress.

www.palgrave.com/pivot

DOI: 10.1057/9781137505903

This book is dedicated to J. & M.,
to my husband Gianpaolo,
to my parents Anna-Clelia and Euclide,
and to my sister Arianna

DOI: 10.1057/9781137505903.0001

Contents

Acknowledgements   vii

Introduction   1

1 Foreign Aid Is Gift   9
   Modernising the order   11
   The Maussian gift   17
   Many gifts   21
   Internationalising the gift   29

2 The Foreign Aid Regime   37
   The new name of peace   38
   Development can be developed   47
   Countries and peoples that cannot be trusted   63
   The logic of the gift   70

3 Dis/Ordering the World   82
   Conflict, poverty and quasi-states   85
   Cooperation, friendship and justice   97
   Conclusion: playing communitas against
      immunitas, and the other way round   108

References   116

Index   131

DOI: 10.1057/9781137505903.0001

Acknowledgements

This work is the result of a process of research and reflection that could not have been possible without the support and input of many colleagues and friends. I am sincerely grateful to Fulvio Cammarano and Igor Pellicciari for having provided the very first stimulus to elaborate around foreign aid as a political practice, and for having continued to sustain such stimulus with the exchange of ideas and the invitation to conferences on the matter. I am also very grateful to Raffaella Baritono for having encouraged me to start putting ideas on paper and for having offered crucial suggestions for the development of the study. I owe the same debt of gratitude to Silvia Vida and Lorenzo Gradoni who have many times shared with me their very precious inputs, have triggered many reflections and have contributed to make this challenging endeavour also a pleasant one. I would like to express my gratitude to Carlo Carini, Raffaella Gherardi, Maurizio Ricciardi and Fausto Proietti for having supported this work from the very beginning, and to Michele Filippini, Lorenzo Fioramonti and the external reviewer at Palgrave Macmillan for their precious preliminary feedback and suggestions. Despite all these valuable contributions, the responsibility of the book's content, including any flaws and omissions that remain, is mine alone. I would like to express my sincere thanks and appreciation to Daniela DeBono for having proofread and copy-edited the manuscript, and to Christina M. Brian, Ambra Finotello and the editorial and production staff at Palgrave Macmillan for their precious professional support.

This work would not have been possible without the support of the Department of Cultural Heritage at the University of Bologna, Ravenna campus, and the continued support of Fondazione Flaminia, particularly of its director Antonio Penso. It would not have been possible without the continued and enriching support of Gustavo Gozzi, whose many professional and personal 'gifts' have been, and will always remain, profoundly inspirational.

DOI: 10.1057/9781137505903.0002

Introduction

Abstract: *This chapter illustrates the main characteristics of the analytical perspective adopted within the study. It starts by comparing this perspective to other approaches dealing with the same matter, and goes on to illustrate the hermeneutical challenges posed by the analysis of foreign aid. 'The Foreign Aid Regime', this chapter argues, represents an original, though preliminary and self-consciously limited, attempt to investigate the specific regime of governmental practices that is established and maintained by and through North–South foreign aid.*

Keywords: development foreign aid; donor/recipient relationship; foreign aid as gift; governmentality; political thought

Furia, Annalisa. *The Foreign Aid Regime: Gift-Giving, States and Global Dis/Order.* Basingstoke: Palgrave Macmillan, 2015. DOI: 10.1057/9781137505903.0003.

Foreign aid is a gift, namely the *voluntary* extension of varied types of resources to foreign peoples. It is presented as a needed gift: as the extension of a *factual*, *material* response to the many persistent plagues that still affect the majority of the world population. As any gift, it suggests taking interest in other peoples. It builds upon the common perception of giving as the duty of the more fortunate and the expression of the highest principles, moral norms and aspirations of the West. It evokes the imagined oneness of the international community, the intention to act for the betterment of a common, shared future. It proliferates upon individuals' commitment, passions and interests. It brings forward hope, the promise of a more equal, free and just international order. Its proclaimed and ever shifting goal is development, that is, to help other people to develop. The main assumption is that development is the catch-all answer to the past and contemporary problems of the South, and that foreign aid is *a necessity*. The main assumption is that *material* resources can trigger development; that the *more* and the *better* foreign aid is given, the *more* likely Southern countries and populations are to improve their condition. The debate on the matter mainly revolves around the adequateness of development goals, framework and strategies, as well as the assessment of aid's accomplishments, deficiencies and technical limitations in a continued call for reform, adjustments and improvements. More crucially, foreign aid is called for; it is not imposed. It is inscribed into the domain of *technical* feasibility, cooperation and moral duty, and not into that of power relations, domination, conflict and exploitation.

In relation to this complex, evocative and powerful phenomenon, this book argues that foreign aid practices constitute a peculiar regime of practices that has evolved over the years from the international government of North–South relations, to the international government of recipient states as well as of selected groups of population *within* and *across* them. Although it is not based on direct, territorial domination or coercion and it does not have the same influence and impact everywhere, foreign aid produces a particular space of international government. A space that is made, and maintained, governable through the operations of the ever-evolving truth, discourse and knowledge of development. A space that is fragmented, loose and selectively inclusive for it is based on *qualitative*, complex and varied aid relationships, even though it is discursively constructed as a unified, *quantitatively* measurable and *technically* manageable and orderable realm. A space in which power relations are not a zero-sum game in which some actors have

DOI: 10.1057/9781137505903.0003

power and some do not have any. A space in which hierarchical relations are maintained *through* the liberty, responsibilisation and active engagement of the governed; through diverse, mobile, intricate and variably flexible spaces of (g)local negotiation and competition as well as (g)local relational networks and alliances. A space in which ownership, participation and good governance have become the appealing words for government and (self-)government. A space in which the need for order is continuously reactivated and it requires variable, dis/ordering forms of intervention, control and monitoring, of categorisation, spatialisation and 'immunisation'.

Particularly central to this analysis are Foucault's notions of 'government' and 'governmentality', which in fact have been used by many authors to investigate and explain the operation and strategic effects of foreign aid. Whereas most interventions on the matter focus with reason on the role played by development discourse and varied technologies, this study attempts to complement these precious contributions by paying specific attention to foreign aid for what it is, namely a new, particular form of *gift* (Hattori 2001). It seeks to demonstrate that it is in particular by analysing the ambiguous nature of foreign aid as gift, as well as the specific dynamic and particular rules of foreign aid relationships as contemporary, international gift-giving relationships, that the intrinsic logic of the foreign aid regime can be addressed in its complexity and *singularity*.

A crucial role in this sense is played by the notion of *debt*. Whereas the creation of debt is a constitutive, dynamic element in the working of any gift-giving practice, being continuously created and erased through giving and counter-giving, in the realm of foreign aid recipient countries' counter-giving is not made *visible*. Their debt cannot be really settled even though it requires continuous, varied and ever shifting 'counter-giving'. Constructed since the very beginning as *unreciprocated, generous* giving practices, such contemporary gift-giving practices have made North–South relations governable by constructing them as relations based on *debt*. They have made recipient countries and populations visible and governable for their material, but also cultural and moral, *indebtedness*, for their substantial *untrustworthiness*. For their continuously renovated and ever-changing *debt* of development.

Whereas the mutual recognition of the donor's and the receiver's identity is a crucial element of any gift-giving practice, in the foreign aid system there is no place left for recipients' plurality of identities and

DOI: 10.1057/9781137505903.0003

diversities. Their *debt* is also a debt of *civilisation* and *culture*. It is also a debt of *capacity* in relation to the donors' varied models, legal and political principles and moral imperatives. A debt that requires and legitimises the continued interference; the *reform* not only of recipient states' inefficient institutions, but also of their societies, and of the behaviour and attitudes of territorial and non-territorial groups of population *within* and *across* them.

More crucially, through foreign aid practices, recipient countries' *debt* of development is constructed – as suggested by the German word for debt (*Schuld*) that means at the same time 'debt' and 'fault' – as both *debt* and *guilt* towards the international community. Debt and liability of *development* that have over the years translated into debt and liability of *sovereignty/security* and hence into debt and liability of *order*.

Contrary to the common conception of foreign aid, this study seeks to demonstrate that beyond the *quantity* of aid, beyond its explicit programmes, paradigms and developmental goals, as well as its factual achievements and failures, it is the *quality* of aid relationships that matters, namely the ambiguous bond that it is created and maintained through the extension of material resources, through the production and renovation of *debt*. It seeks to demonstrate that the objective of foreign aid practices, their intrinsic logic, is to perpetuate this bond.

Contrary to the binary interpretations of foreign aid practices as a foreign policy tool to preserve hierarchical power relations and security in an intrinsically anarchical international domain, or as an ethical tool to promote development and cooperation and contribute to a more equitable international order, commonly provided for by political realism and liberal internationalism, this volume seeks to demonstrate that the foreign aid regime's effects cannot be captured by remaining within the classical divide between *conservation* and *transformation*, between *domination* and *freedom*. It seeks to demonstrate that foreign aid practices allow the *conservation* of order, hierarchy and inequality because they operate *through* the freedom, active engagement and responsibilisation of recipients; they operate through a *material and ethical promise* of *transformation*, of a new order, freedom and equality. They allow the conservation of the existing relations of interdependence by continuously promising the construction of new relations of inter-dependence, that are always *yet-to-come*.

The book is structured in the following manner. Chapter 1 of the book is an investigation into the peculiar history of the concept of gift, showing

DOI: 10.1057/9781137505903.0003

what has led to its demotion in the modernised economic and political domain as well as its many possible interpretations and intrinsic epistemological challenges. Looking at the ways in which the notion of gift may apply to international relations, the chapter illustrates why foreign aid is to be interpreted as a particular, new form of gift that produces a particular, new regime of practices which is not comparable with traditional, existing models of gift-giving practices and which thus requires to be investigated anew. The chapter concludes with the illustration of the specific analytical perspective adopted for the investigation of such contemporary regime of practices, that is the 'analytics of government' as elaborated by Dean (2010).

Chapter 2 investigates the foreign aid regime by scrutinising its truth, discourse and knowledge, its explicit aims and programmes for reform and the ways in which its constitutive actors and institutions interact, are constructed, are made visible and are entrusted with authority. Adopting a historical perspective, the chapter illustrates how the foreign aid regime has emerged after the Second World War as a regime of practices of international government of North–South relations and how it has increasingly expanded to encompass not only a regime of government of Southern countries but also selected groups within and across them. Through the investigation of its multilevel operations, the chapter highlights that the intrinsic logic and strategy of foreign aid regime is to be found in the ambivalence, or the 'double bind' that is inherent to any gift-giving practice.

Chapter 3 investigates in which ways the notion of sovereignty together with its shifting conceptions form part of the foreign aid regime governmental rationality. Distinguishing between the conservative/conflictual and the transformative/cooperative potential intrinsic to any gift-giving practices, the chapter then applies these categories to analyse primarily the ways in which foreign aid practices have been interpreted but also how themes such as poverty, inequality and the obligation to extend aid have been constructed and put into practice in the foreign aid regime. By applying the same categories to the notions of communitas/immunitas, order/disorder, the chapter shows how the foreign aid regime proliferates through the continuous interplay between the one(s) and the other(s).

This study is the result of a process of theoretical reflection around some of the themes and motifs that have come to be connected with the foreign aid endeavour such as human rights theory and practice, human development and human security. It is also the result of the experience gained through five years of professional collaboration with the Italian branch of an international NGO. Although not directly related to the foreign aid field, such a rich and complex personal and professional journey outside the academic world has allowed me to directly experience the complex relationships that exist among funding agencies, recipient intermediaries and final beneficiaries.

The methodology adopted within this study is based on two major axes. First is the scrutiny of the theoretical roots of the concept of aid seen as a necessary starting point for the analysis of the power relations that are established and perpetuated by and through foreign aid practices. This line of investigation, which identifies in the gift the conceptual equivalent of foreign aid, was inspired by Hattori's (2001, 2003) highly valuable, pioneering reflection on the matter. The second axis is the investigation of foreign aid practices as a particular regime of practices of government. This second line of investigation draws inspiration from Dean's (2010) very precious illustration of the 'analytics of government' perspective. Another highly valuable source of inspiration is represented by Duffield's contributions on aid as a liberal system of global governance and on the impact of the reshaping of the development–security nexus on foreign aid governmental rationality (in particular 2001a, 2001b, 2002, 2007).

These main axes of analysis are complemented, in Chapter 3, by the investigation of the ways in which the notion of sovereignty together with its shifting conceptions are the necessary conditions for the operation of the foreign aid regime and form part of its governmental rationality. This represents yet another level at which the effects of the foreign aid regime become visible, productive and intersect with other regimes of international government such as those which Simpson (2004) defines the 'criminal law regime' and the 'democratic governance regime'. This final part of the study is inspired by Simpson's work.

While due and necessary, the acknowledgement of the intellectual 'debts' contracted with this study – and debt is a proper term in a work that elaborates around the concept of gift – also emphasises why foreign aid is still a field which, in spite of being politically productive, remains substantially unexplored by political thought scholars. A possible reason for this is that foreign aid represents a crucial hermeneutical challenge for political thought. The first reason is that foreign aid challenges and peculiarly reshapes the traditional divide between *war* and *commerce* – conflict and cooperation – that are the classical, broad categories through which

DOI: 10.1057/9781137505903.0003

Western political thought conceptualises the relations between states. The second reason is that even though it started as a political practice, and indeed its political origins, motives and effects have been analysed and intensely debated, foreign aid is still predominantly presented as a *technical* task within the domain of economic and social sciences. As such it is still discursively located within the realm of *policy* rather than *politics*. Thirdly, its conceptual roots sink into a notion (that of the gift) that in Western political thought has been considered, starting from the modern age, as intrinsically *apolitical*. Finally, foreign aid is a complex, varied and multidimensional set of governmental *practices* whose operations and effects are not fully understandable by analysing the role of institutions, particular ideologies, concepts or doctrines.

The simple reference to these limitations and challenges, to which many others could be added, is sufficient to explain why this study can be legitimately presented as a preliminary and consciously limited attempt to investigate foreign aid practices as constituting a particular regime of practices of international government. The necessity to draw from a composite assemblage of different analytical perspectives has often entailed proceeding along an impervious path that moves across many methodological traps and difficulties. It has also required a careful limitation of the investigation.

The study has in fact several limitations. Firstly, the investigation is *culturally* and *spatially* limited as it focuses only on donors' prevailing practices and thinking, and on North–South relations as the first domain in which such regime of practices has historically emerged. This is the case in spite of the reality that foreign aid practices have informed West–East relations, as also East–South, South–South and East–East relations. Secondly, this study focuses on that which is called 'development foreign aid', and it does not address the particular types of practices that are commonly referred to as 'humanitarian aid' and 'codevelopment'. Whereas some of the outcomes of this study are probably relevant also for the study of these practices, and the literature on humanitarian aid has in part informed its development, the scrutiny of their specific logic requires a set of specifications that are not within the scope of this investigation. The third limitation is linked to the use of the terms 'South', 'Third World', 'developing countries' or 'recipient countries', which are used knowingly in spite of the pejorative meaning with which they have been infused in development discourse. Their use in this study is maintained in order to emphasise that their formation is an integral component of the operation

DOI: 10.1057/9781137505903.0003

of the foreign aid regime. Similarly, the vague terms 'West' and 'North', as well as the related adjectives, are used to also emphasise the ways in which the us/them division is maintained and reshaped by foreign aid practices. Finally, this study might be considered limited also because it does not prescribe adjustments, possible reforms or new programmes to follow. Rather its main aim is, in line with the intents of an analytics of government, to attempt to contribute to the understanding of the *contingent, historical* and *situated* nature of the foreign aid regime, what intrinsic logic is constitutive of foreign aid practices and what their strategic effects are (see Dean 2010: 45–50). The hope is that this could contribute to a critical, rigorous thinking about the dangers that shadow what, following Miller and Rose (1990), we could term as our 'will to give'. The hope is that this could enhance the possibility of *thinking* and *acting* in different, new ways, and contribute to make us more *responsible* when we continue to think and act in the same ways (see Dean 2010: 45–50).

DOI: 10.1057/9781137505903.0003

1
Foreign Aid Is Gift

Abstract: *The concept of gift is a precious hermeneutical tool that serves to analyse the notion of foreign aid and its practices. Using as a starting point the analysis of the history of this concept, the chapter draws attention to its demotion in the modernised economic and political domain, and to its many possible interpretations and intrinsic epistemological challenges. By looking at the ways in which the notion of gift may be of use in international relations, Furia argues that foreign aid constitutes an international gift that produces a particular regime of practices that is not comparable with the existing models of gift-giving practices. 'Foreign Aid Is a Gift' concludes with an illustration of the specific methodology adopted for the investigation of this contemporary regime of practices.*

Keywords: analytics of government; concept/practice of gift; gift in modern state and market; Maussian gift

Furia, Annalisa. *The Foreign Aid Regime: Gift-Giving, States and Global Dis/Order.* Basingstoke: Palgrave Macmillan, 2015. DOI: 10.1057/9781137505903.0004.

Since the publication of the seminal essay *The Gift* by Marcel Mauss (1923–4, *L'Année Sociologique*), the investigation of the many ramifications, constitutive ambiguities and multiple potentialities of the concept, as well as the practice of gift, has engaged scholars across disciplines. Since then, anthropologists, sociologists and philosophers from diverse theoretical approaches and continents have engaged with Mauss's argumentations. Classicists, historians of varied periods and specialisations, literary scholars, Marxist theorists, theologians and economists have turned to the field re-opened by Mauss's work and incorporated its insights into their own fields (Liebersohn 2011: 4). The recent resurgence of interest in the world of the gift has further expanded its already blurred boundaries over feminist studies, aesthetics, literary, film and art criticism, ethics, and has relentlessly nurtured current reflections on disparate themes within, across and at the intersection of a number of disciplines – from discourses around 'feminine' economies and post-capitalist market economy to regulations on corporate and government ethics on gift-giving, and from feminist analyses of motherhood to ethical investigation of blood and organ donation (see for instance Guenther 2006, Moore 2011, Zamagni and Bruni 2013).

Not satisfied with remaining within the domestic borders, interest in the Maussian gift has also spilled over into the international domain. While its sole name whispers of something *different*, of the possibility of a radical and elusive alternative to that which Dardot and Laval term the neo-liberal 'normative system' and its founding 'global rationality' (2013), the investigation of the troubled history and of the current life of the concept of gift shows however that there is not a 'universality of gift', neither in its conceptualisation, nor in its practice (Carlà and Gori 2014: 22). Ethnographically and historically situated in time and in place, its practice has always variously crossed different domains and has unfolded according to diverse rules. The discourses around it have been variously constructed and fraught with fluctuating functions and meanings. Its varied conceptualisations have emerged from the diverse theoretical domains the gift intersects and have divergently focused on the *subjective* intentions of its actors, on the *objective* nature of thing that is given, and on the process that is activated by the act of giving, or on a variable conjugation of all (or of some) of these components.

Although it needs to be handled with great caution, I argue that the concept of gift provides the right entry point to the conceptual understanding of foreign aid and to the scrutiny of foreign aid practices. With

DOI: 10.1057/9781137505903.0004

the aim of historically contextualising the emergence of the concept of gift and of substantiating its relevance for the case at stake, the first three sections of this chapter provide a critical investigation of the gift's particular history, hermeneutical potential and many pitfalls based on the wide literature on the matter. The fourth section investigates the ways in which the concept of gift has been applied to the analysis of international relations and practices and it delineates the analytical framework adopted within the scope of the study.

Modernising the order

> *Omnis determinatio est negatio.*
> *(Spinoza)*

Practices of gift-giving, along with reflection on the nature and various meanings attributed to the gift, as well as narratives and moral instruction 'in the art of giving and receiving', have always been associated with Western civilisation (Liebersohn 2011: 3). Indeed, it is widely acknowledged that Judeo-Christian ethical and religious norms and rituals, Roman poetry, law and ethical thinking, and Greek philosophy and tragedy are the primary (and some times competing) sources of most of the nuances and meanings that still substantiate the contemporary concept of gift (Osteen 2002, Davis 2014). Over the centuries, traditional gift-giving practices have been reiterated and re-invented. Ancestral meanings attached to them have been preserved and reshaped depending on the specific needs, concrete conditions and conventions/principles regulating each geographical context and each domain of life.[1] To borrow Athané's efficacious expression, not only has the concept of gift contributed to making our history, but it has also been continuously made and re-made by our history (2008: 325). In this long history, an important turning point is represented by the affirmation of the idea that gift-giving practices produce and are part of a distinct and somehow unified realm. This is an assumption that still informs the contemporary conceptions of gifts and is one of the most important products of the late modern history of the concept of gift (Davis 2014). In brief, while the concept of gift flowed 'freely' in the ancient world, medieval and early modern societies – variously informing disparate aspects of their political, religious, social and economic life – it gained its contemporary

DOI: 10.1057/9781137505903.0004

conceptual *positioning* (which does not mean clarity or certainty) by being *conceptually* (certainly not practically) limited and constrained, and by increasingly losing its pre-modern freedom of movement. Freedom of movement that found expression in disparate forms and places: from ancient *euergetism* and *leitourgeia*, to medieval and modern liberality obligations of lords, noblemen and sovereigns; from the upward flux of tribute from subjects to their masters, to that from noblemen to sovereigns; from Christian moralisation and interiorisation of gift-giving practices, to the role of the church as receiver of charitable donations and instrument for extending charity; from the meaning and function of alms and donations to the poor, to the gift's inherence in various forms of 'acquisition, alienation and exchange' (Carlà and Gori 2014: 16, Athané 2008, Davis 2014).

Whereas the practice of gift-giving has continued to inform life within societies, the concept of gift paradoxically gained its peculiar *positioning* as a result of the long and complex process that led to the *devaluation* of both its role and its contribution to the construction, operation and stability of the modern Western political and economic order.[2] Even though such a process of 'modernisation' extended over many years, and involved many aspects and institutions, two classical examples of its main characteristics can be found in the role Thomas Hobbes and Adam Smith assigned to the concept of gift in their theoretical constructions.

Hobbes addresses the definition and the function of the gift in several passages of *De Cive* (1642), as well as in his more famous and mature work, the *Leviathan* (1651). In addition to the many passages in which the practice of gift is traditionally framed as a form of worship, as connected to the virtue of liberality, and as a means to honour a person and to procure friends and servants (for example, see *Leviathan*, XXXI, XII, XV and X), Hobbes develops his *rational* construction of the modern order by contrasting the *contract* upon which such an order is to be built to the concept of gift, as illustrated by the following passages of chapter XIV of *Leviathan*:

> The mutual transferring of right, is that which men call CONTRACT. [...]
>
> When the transferring of Right is not mutuall, but one of the Parties transferreth in hope to gain thereby friendship or service from another, or from his friends; or in hope to gain the reputation of Charity, or Magnanimity; or to deliver his mind from the pain of compassion; or in hope of reward in heaven; This is not Contract, but GIFT, FREE GIFT, GRACE: which words signifie one and the same thing. [...]

DOI: 10.1057/9781137505903.0004

But there is between these two sorts of merit this difference, that in contract I merit by virtue of my own power and the contractor's need; but in this case of free gift, I am enabled to merit only by the benignity of the giver: in contract, I merit at the contractor's hand that he should depart with his right; in this case of gift, I merit not that the giver should part with his right; but that when he has parted with it, it should be mine rather than another's. And this I think to be the meaning of that distinction of the Schools between *meritum congrui* and *meritum condigni*. (Hobbes 1839[1651]: 120–1,123–4)

To be more precise, that upon which Hobbes erects the rational and artificial political order that will grant safety and peace to men is not a contract but a *pact* or *covenant*. Although the concept of contract implies the mutual transfer of rights, with the concept of pact or covenant Hobbes highlights the need to create the conditions to ensure not only such a transfer, but also its projection into the future and therefore its continuity over time (see *Leviathan*, XIV). It is thus from such a *pactum unionis*, from 'the men united by consent', that the Leviathan, which is external to such a pact and is created through it, receives all men's natural rights (except the right of self-defence) and acquires the 'greatest of human powers' (Hobbes 1839[1651]: 74, chapter X). Namely, the power that is necessary to avoid the war of all against all, to deliver '*the safety of the people*' and to provide the establishment and preservation of the *artificial* domestic order (Hobbes 1839[1651]: 322, chapter XXX). With regard to such a political project, the concept of gift is considered a unilateral 'transferring of right' that does not produce any obligation, does not give rise to any *due* action and does not ensure any temporal continuity. As such, it cannot play any relevant role, even though it carries some residual functions. With the aim of rationalising political theory and practice, and radically breaking with the preceding political and legal tradition, Hobbes rejects any idea of *political* productivity of the gift. Due to the uncertainty, instability and risk it entails, the gift cannot usefully serve the cause of pacification and of incorporation of self-interested individuals *who distrust each other* into a single political entity. The gift cannot provide grounds for the establishment of mutual obligation. It can be part of the modern political domain only insofar as it relates to one of the *moral* virtues necessary for peaceful coexistence, as Hobbes highlights in the description of the fourth law of nature, *gratitude*:

As justice dependeth on antecedent covenant; so does GRATITUDE depend on antecedent grace; that is to say, antecedent free gift: and is the fourth law of nature, which may be conceived in this form, *that a man which receiveth benefit*

DOI: 10.1057/9781137505903.0004

from another of mere grace, endeavour that he which giveth it, have no reasonable cause to repent him of his good will. For no man giveth, but with intention of good to himself; because gift is voluntary; and of all voluntary acts, the object is to every man his own good; of which if men see they shall be frustrated, there will be no beginning of benevolence, or trust; nor consequently of mutual help; nor of reconciliation of one man to another; and therefore they are to remain still in the condition of *war*, which is contrary to the first and fundamental law of nature, which commandeth men *to seek peace*. (Hobbes 1839[1651]: 138, chapter XV)

In Smith's reflection, the continuous and difficult attempt to account for both the social and self-interested inclination of individuals occupies a central place and has been the object of a deep investigation and tense debates amongst scholars. Commonly known as the 'Adam Smith problem', such a 'problem' has traditionally been defined in terms of a radical contradiction – a theoretical inconsistency between a moral theory based on the 'sympathetic part of human nature' and a market theory based on 'its selfish part' (Buckle quoted in Raphael and Macfie 1982:21). Evidence of this inconsistency would be, on the one hand, the moral value Smith assigns to *benevolence* in his account of ethics and human behaviour in *The Theory of Moral Sentiments* (1759); and, on the other hand, the dismissive treatment benevolence receives in his well-known economic text, *The Wealth of Nations* (1776). In this regard, the widely quoted and famous passage of *The Wealth of Nations*, hereafter proposed, is generally reported as the major piece of evidence of such a supposed radical change:

It is not from the benevolence of the butcher, the brewer, or the baker, that we expect our dinner, but from their regard to their own interest. We address ourselves, not to their humanity, but to their self-love, and never talk to them of our own necessities, but of their advantages. (Smith 2007[1776]: 9–10)

What is relevant for the purposes of this study is that, whereas many studies have highlighted the different focus, consistency and substantial complementarity between the two writings (Raphael and Macfie 1982, Offer 1997, Birch 1998, Min 2002), it seems correct to say that in Smith's economic theory it is the exchange of commodities based upon individual self-interest that is the best guarantee of social bond. In this context, the need for benevolence is deemed to be irrelevant to the working and expansion of prudent and just capitalist behaviour in a competitive free-market commercial society (Rist 2008: 18, Birch

DOI: 10.1057/9781137505903.0004

1998: 35–6). Smith recognises the function of some acts of liberality and hospitality from a historical perspective in his economic masterpiece. He acknowledges and analyses the rationality of benevolent acts in pre-modern, pre-commercial and pre-manufacturing societies whereas in his analysis of benevolent acts in the modern commercial society he either accommodates them within market terms, or connects them with ill-judged actions and policies, or else considers them as an emotional interference   (Liebersohn 2011: 36–7, Birch 1998: 25, 35). In Smith's perspective, giving gifts, that is, being benevolent, is not relevant to a market economy because it does not form a *dignified* and *constitutive* part of the operations of a rational market based on individual self-interest, and regulated by both institutional infrastructures and settings and by the *invisible hand*:

> As every individual, therefore, endeavours as much as he can, both to employ his capital in the support of domestic industry, and so to direct that industry that its produce maybe of the greatest value; every individual necessarily labours to render the annual revenue of the society as great as he can. He generally, indeed, *neither intends to promote the public interest*, nor knows *how much he is promoting it*. By preferring the support of domestic to that of foreign industry, he intends only his own security; and by directing that industry in such a manner as its produce may be of the greatest value, he intends only his own gain; and he is in this, as in many other cases, *led by an invisible hand to promote an end which was no part of his intention*. Nor is it always the worse for the society that it was no part of it. By pursuing his own interest, he frequently promotes that of the society more effectually than when he really intends to promote it. (Smith 2007[1776]: 293, emphasis added)

However, as effectively highlighted by Liebersohn, gift-giving practices may persist within a modern commercial society, as a complement, as a consequence of the wealth and the social bound produced by commerce (Liebersohn 2011: 38, Min 2002: 134). In this regard, in her foreword to the English edition of Mauss's *The Gift*, Douglas for instance emphasises that:

> The gift cycle echoes Adam Smith's invisible hand: *gift complements market in so far as it operates where the latter is absent*. Like the market it supplies each individual with personal incentives for collaborating in the pattern of exchanges. Gifts are given in a context of public drama, with nothing secret about them. In being more directly cued to public esteem, the distribution of honour, and the sanctions of religion, the gift economy is more visible than the market. Just by being visible, the resultant distribution of goods and

DOI: 10.1057/9781137505903.0004

services is more readily subject to public scrutiny and judgements of fairness than are the results of market exchange. (2002: xviii, emphasis added)

In this sense, whereas the market is the realm of commutative justice, impartiality and indifference, the world of the gift is the *distinct* but *complementary* realm of distributive justice, desire for approbation and others' 'favourable regard', personal relations and moral virtues (see Offer 1997, Min 2002).

The most evident effect of the long, non-unidirectional and varied historical process exemplified by the briefly sketched reflections around the state and the market economy given earlier – which of course would include many other theoretical perspectives – is the fact that it has been made impossible to think again of the gift as a modern *politically* and *economically* productive concept. As a *dignified* component of life and not as a concept that is substantially defined *per differentiam*: as a non contract-based, non-regulated transfer of goods and services that does not have a deontic structure (Athané 2008: 236); as an action that is not informed by market's impersonality, equality and symmetry, nor by commutative justice's neutrality and indifference to diversity (Brezzi 2011: 12–14). Whereas the modern state creates *homo aequalis*, the market bases its functioning on *homo oeconomicus*, and no relevant place is left for the *homo donator* (Godbout 2006: 91).

It is thus not a case that the more effectively confined 'behind the market and the state' (Godbout and Caillé 1998: 13), the concept of gift disappears, with very few exceptions, from the writings of European thinkers from around the end of the Napoleonic period to the end of the First World War, when it was *recovered* by Mauss (Liebersohn 2011: 3). The 'victory of rationalism and mercantilism' (Mauss 2002[1923–4]: 97), the imperious consecration of the model of rational, self-interested, utilitarian individuals immersed in ever-developing and expanding capitalist market economies and bureaucratic nation–states which was started and favoured by the European project of political modernity, forced the vividness of gift-giving practices, which had never ceased to exist, into the realm of the *implicit*, making their contribution seem *irrelevant* to structure the national order (Liebersohn 2011: 5). Of the complex and varied world of meanings and functions the gift had embodied, only the idea, and ideal, of the *pure*, unilateral, free and voluntary gift survived within the Western modernised world. In other parts of the world, when detected as a structural component of economics, politics and society, gift-exchange was discarded as 'an ignoble form of exchange', as bribery

DOI: 10.1057/9781137505903.0004

that could only exist in primitive, inferior and archaic societies (2011: 167). At the beginning of the twentieth century, after a century of practical *persistence* coupled with theoretical *neglect*, the attention towards the concept of gift and the role of gift-exchange practices started to flourish again, this time in new forms as a result of encounters with life outside the borders of the West (2011: 7). As highlighted by Liebersohn in his intriguing account of the vicissitudes of the gift throughout the history of Western civilisation, it was the European overseas travellers and, more importantly, the fathers of modern anthropology (Boas, Malinowski) who recovered the gift 'at the colonial margins' and 'brought it back' to the Western rationalised societies (2011: 6, 7). And it was by drawing both on new ethnographic evidence gathered by anthropologists and travellers, as well as on notions already developed by historians of ancient German law and language (see Magnani 2007), that Mauss could develop his highly suggestive work on the concept of the gift.

The Maussian gift

> *The saying goes 'gifts persuade the gods'.*
>
> (Euripides, Medea, line 963)

In his investigation of the varied systems of contractual law and economic exchanges that characterised some ethnographic areas of Polynesia, Melanesia and North-West America, traces of which he also found in Roman, German and other Indo-European ancient laws and custom, Mauss develops an *evolutive* account of gift-exchange. According to him, the practice of gift-exchange, neglected in contemporary societies due to the expansion of market systems, is to be recognised as inherent to Western tradition and acknowledged as a foundational and *recurring* phenomenon across diverse cultures and historical periods. It is to be newly given value for transmitting the values, attitudes and organisational procedures that define 'the path that our nations must follow, both in their morality and in their economy' (2002[1923–4]: 100). As he says in the last pages of his work:

> It is our western societies who have recently made man an 'economic animal'. But we are not yet all creatures of this genus. [...] *Homo oeconomicus* is not behind us, but lies ahead, as does the man of morality and duty, the man of

DOI: 10.1057/9781137505903.0004

science and reason. For a very long time man was something different, and he has not been a machine for very long, made complicated by a calculating machine. (Mauss 2002[1923–4]: 98)

Actively engaged in the socialist, solidarist and cooperative movements of his time (see Mallard 2010), he promotes the need to return to the 'very principle of normal social life', which consists in every domain, of 'a good but moderate blend of reality and the ideal'. A return of the moral inclination to simultaneously take into consideration one's own self-interest and the interests of society (2002[1923–4]: 89, 88). Moral inclination, an 'eternal' morality that according to Mauss is common to all in past, present and future societies, and that has its origins in the archaic system of 'total services', in the system of gift-exchange he investigates (2002[1923–4]: 89–90).[3]

From the outset, he clarifies the intention to focus on a particular set of phenomena and on its main characteristic, that is:

the so to speak voluntary character of these total services, apparently *free* and *disinterested* but nevertheless *constrained* and *self-interested*. Almost always such services have taken the form of the gift, the present generously given even when, in the gesture accompanying the transaction, there is only a *polite fiction, formalism, and social deceit*, and when really there *is obligation and economic self-interest*. (Mauss 2002[1923–4]: 4, emphasis added)

Mauss therefore focuses on transactions, exchanges that even when involving individuals are carried on by collective bodies, legal entities such as clan, tribes, families and groups 'who confront and oppose one another' and exchange:

not solely property and wealth, movable and immovable goods, and things economically useful. In particular, such exchanges are acts of politeness: banquets, rituals, military services, women, children, dances, festivals, and fairs, *in which economic transaction is only one element*, and in which the passing on of wealth is only one feature of a much more general and *enduring contract*. (Mauss 2002[1923–4]: 6–7, emphasis added)

Offering an insight that has drained scholars for years, Mauss affirms that the services and the counter-services that constitute gift-exchange practices, although disguised in the form of *voluntary* acts, are intrinsically and strictly *obligatory*, 'on pain of private or public warfare' (2002[1923–4]: 7). According to Mauss gift-exchange carries with it a set of obligations: the obligation to reciprocate gifts, but also the obligation to give and to receive gifts. The obligation to *give* is the essence of *potlatch*, a complex

DOI: 10.1057/9781137505903.0004

gift-giving ceremony practised in various forms by many tribes of Pacific Northwest coast, Alaska and California whose recurring elements are the giving away or destruction of long-stored goods in a guest–host setting 'for the issue of title setting' and for *recognition* of the host/giver's title and status (Risdale 2011: 7 quoting Drucker). In Mauss's analysis the potlatch represents the extreme, agonist form of gift exchange, for it is a 'struggle of wealth'. It includes elements of competition, rivalry and excess aimed at ensuring that the chief of the host tribe can keep his authority and secure his superior position by displaying his fortune, by creating obligations that cannot be repaid, and in some cases by humiliating the chief of the guest tribe (2002[1923–4]: 47, 47–50).

According to Mauss's analysis, the distribution of goods at a potlatch and in every occasion of importance is closely related to the notion of *honour,* is held to mark political (and every kind of) *rank* and is the fundamental act to ensure *public recognition* in the military, economic, legal and religious spheres. More generally, failing to invite someone to a potlatch is a failure to give and therefore 'tantamount to declaring war' as one would be rejecting 'the bond of alliance and commonality' (2002[1923–4]: 17). Similarly, the refusal of a gift, or the refusal to attend a potlatch, is an expression of fear of 'losing one's name'. Or rather, it is 'to admit oneself beaten in advance', and it is only in very few cases that it may happen to be an assertion of victory and superiority (2002[1923–4]: 52). Finally, the obligation to reciprocate 'with interest' is essential to gift and to potlatch, except when the potlatch involves pure destruction and is carried out by a superior clan, or by a clan already recognised as superior (2002[1923–4]: 53). The sanction for not worthily returning a gift (or a potlatch) is the loss of *rank*, of 'face' and results in enslavement for *debt* (2002[1923–4]: 54). In Mauss's account, a gift necessarily implies the notion of *credit* that according to him was known also in archaic societies. This sharply contrasts with what was affirmed by many jurists and economists who imagined an evolution from primitive societies based on barter to more advanced ones based on sales for cash, scaling up to a higher phase of civilisation that would be characterised by sale on credit. On the contrary, according to Mauss, the notion of credit, on the one hand, is part of every 'primitive' society and, on the other hand, barter, purchase, sale and loan systems are derived from a simplification of the discontinuous temporality inherent to gift-exchange practices. Not to constitute a refusal, an offence, a gift in fact cannot be immediately reciprocated, but there should be a *time lapse* between the act of giving and the act of returning. On the contrary, barter, buying and selling arose, according to Mauss, by simplifying, reducing and fixing the time limit implied by the gift, which was formerly arbitrary (2002[1923–4]: 45–6).

By continuing to draw from various examples derived from ethnographic research and ancient literature, Mauss highlights also the intrinsic *power* of the thing given. This power derives from the intrinsic spirit of the thing that is given 'without setting a price on it', from the famous *hau* of the Maori. It is the *hau* of the gift – that 'wishes to return to its birthplace [...], and to the owner' – that makes the object given a part of the donor's identity, nature and spiritual essence (2002[1923–4]: 14–15). It also makes it not only illicit but also *dangerous* to keep the object given without repaying it with something that can take its place, or without circulating it. As he explains in relation to the working of the *hau*:

> to accept something from somebody is to accept some part of his spiritual essence, of his soul. To retain that thing would be dangerous and mortal, not only because it would be against law and morality, but also because that thing coming from the person not only morally, but physically and spiritually, that essence, that food, those goods, whether movable or immovable [...] – all exert a magical or religious hold over you. (2002[1923–4]: 16).

Therefore making a gift of something is 'to make a present of some part of oneself'. Gifts themselves forge 'a bilateral, irrevocable bond' between the donor and the recipient who become dependent on each other, and in this sense they imply an existential *danger*[4] (2002 [1923–4]: 16, 76). In this context, gift-exchange represents 'an intermingling', where souls and things, persons and things, 'each emerges from their own sphere and mixes together' (2002[1923–4]: 25–6).

Gift-exchange practices also have a 'mythical, religious and magical aspect'. They are connected with sacrifice, with relations between men and gods, with sacred beings, nature and also with the dead who are seen as the real owners of the world's wealth and whose favour and consent has to be bought (2002[1923–4]: 30,18–22).

The main argument with Mauss's analysis is in fact that gift transactions are '*total* social facts': in some forms they involve the 'totality of society and its institutions', in other cases, when the exchange concerns individuals, they involve 'a very large number of institutions'. In any case, they are considered 'at the same time juridical, economic, religious, and even aesthetic and morphological'. They concern private and public law, the religious sphere and mentality in a strict sense, and economic notions.

DOI: 10.1057/9781137505903.0004

They partake of the political sphere and they are 'structural', because, they take place during assemblies, fairs, markets, and they presuppose 'tribal, intertribal or international alliances, those of the *commercium* and the *connubium*'. They are more than single themes or institutions, and even more than a system of institutions – they are 'whole "entities"', concrete, ever-evolving and living facts (2002[1923–4]: 100–2).

More importantly, they are the expression, as Mauss highlights in his concluding remarks, of the ways in which societies themselves, their subgroups and in the end their individual members, have progressed in 'substituting alliance, gifts, and trade for war, isolation and stagnation'; in 'stabilizing relationships'; and in 'exchanging goods and persons, no longer only between clans, but between tribes and nations, and, above all, between individuals' (2002[1923–4]: 105–6). Gift-giving practices are the expression of the ways in which people had learnt in ancient times, and should also relearn in contemporary ones, to build *mutual trust*:

> to create mutual interests, giving mutual satisfaction, and, in the end, to defend them without having to resort to arms. [...] to *oppose* and to *give* to one another without *sacrificing* themselves to one another. (Mauss 2002[1923–4]: 106, emphasis added)

Many gifts

> *A man's gift makes room for him,*
> *And brings him before great men.*
>
> (*Proverbs, 18:16*)

It has been observed that Mauss's essay on the gift speaks about many things apart from the gift (Derrida 1992:24, see also Laidlaw 2002: 56–7). The conceptualisation propounded by Mauss, which represents an unavoidable point of reference for any subsequent reflection on the matter, seems in fact to be in sharp contrast with the idea of gift as a *free* gift, as the result of a sincerely benevolent, unconstrained, purely altruistic *intention*, as is reflected in its commonsense use.[5] The possibility of conceiving, and even more so extending, such a *pure* gift is a dense and intense question, amongst the many others that still baffles any reasoning around the universe of the gift. According to Derrida, the only possible meaning of the gift derives from the giver's intention:

DOI: 10.1057/9781137505903.0004

> There is no gift without the intention of giving. The gift can only have a meaning that is intentional – in the two senses of the word that refers to intention as well as intentionality. However, everything stemming from the intentional meaning also threatens the gift with self-keeping, with being kept in its very expenditure. (1992: 123)

In this sense, in his famous philosophical inquiry into the matter Derrida defines the gift as '*the* impossible. The very figure of the impossible' for the gift carries with it an intrinsic '*double bind*': 'For there to be gift, it is necessary that the gift not even appear, that it not be perceived or received as gift' (1992: 7, 16). As he further explains:

> For there to be a gift, *it is necessary* that the donnee not give back, amortize, reimburse, acquit himself, enter into a contract, and that he never have contracted a debt. [...] It is thus necessary, at the limit, that he not *recognize* the gift as gift. [...] the one who gives it must not see it or know it [...]; otherwise he begins, at the threshold, as soon as he intends to give, to pay himself with a symbolic recognition, to praise himself, [...] to congratulate himself, to give back to himself symbolically the value of what he thinks he has given or what is preparing to give. [...] The truth of the gift [...] suffices to annul the gift. The truth of the gift is equivalent to the non-gift or to the non-truth of the gift. (1992: 13–14, 27)

Describing transactions that are 'serious politics and serious economics' (Laidlaw 2002: 57), Mauss's account of gift relates in a complex way with the 'double bind' of gift, as well as with the idea of the pure gift and with the opaque domain of the giver's *intention*. According to Laidlaw's interesting interpretation, the Maussian gift can be at the same time free and not free, a point that was frequently highlighted by the same Mauss, because it is based on the continuous invocation of the idea of the free gift which the reader surely has, but it does not include any attempt to define or further explore the idea of the free gift. Laidlaw submits that by analysing the *hau* Mauss makes appeal to the common understanding of the gift as something that is always personal and *intentional*, and in this way he can explain why and how it is that gifts can create the moral basis of sociality. On the other hand, by highlighting the intrinsic connection of gifts with calculation, self-interest and obligation, also commonly experienced in everyday life and contemporary practices of gift, Mauss revaluates their capacity to contain conflict and to fruitfully combine competition and opposition with pacification and cooperation (2002: 56–8). It is this 'rhetorical double movement' that makes it possible to understand the gift as a combination of obligation and freedom (2002:

DOI: 10.1057/9781137505903.0004

57). As Laidlaw further highlights, 'gifts evoke obligations and create reciprocity, but they can do this because they might not' (2002: 58).

Within the context of his account of the concepts of *habitus* and of *symbolic* capital, Bourdieu discusses, in numerous interventions (see 1990, 1998), the question of gift as 'a paradigm of the economy of symbolic goods' (1998: 98). In Bourdieu's perspective, key to understand gift-exchange is the determinant role that is played by the temporal interval that must occur between the gift and the counter-gift. Whereas an immediate reciprocation would be interpreted in all societies as a refusal, the time interval is necessary precisely to permit both the giver and the receiver to experience the gift as gratuitous and not obligatory. On the giver's part, the interval signifies the uncertainty, the risk that the gift will not be reciprocated. On the receiver's part, it signifies that the counter-gift is free, not determined by the initial gift (1998:94). In this sense, the temporal structure of the gift allows the coexistence of a 'subjective truth and a quite opposite objective truth' (1990:107). It serves to mask, to repress for the actors involved and for all the others, the fact that such an 'individual *self-deception*, is sustained by a collective *self-deception*, a veritable *collective misrecognition*' inscribed in mental, historical and objective structures of society that makes it impossible to think and act otherwise (1998:95). In Bourdieu's theory of action, rather than being understood through a focus on the *intention* of the agents, practices of gift-exchange, just like many other human actions, are to be investigated through the concept of *habitus* – 'acquired dispositions', internalised and socialised rules that work to transfigure their truth. For Bourdieu gift-exchange is based on ritualised and imposed forms, on formalities and euphemisms, such as the time interval and, more broadly, on 'socially constituted "collective expectations"'. In this way the economic domination implied by gift-giving, the *objective* truth of the gift 'as an economic exchange' practice, can be denied (1998: 102, 99, 98). According to Bourdieu, every gift, even the most benevolent and *equal*, but even more so the *unequal* ones, implies, through the work-ing of the logic of debt and of its peculiar temporal structure, a certain degree of 'symbolic domination' understood as 'relations of domination based on communication, knowledge and recognition' which are based on common categories of perception and appreciation (1998: 100). In this sense, according to Bourdieu every gift is '*possessive*', as it aims at increasing the donor's *symbolic capital*.[6] It is also *illusive* as the common perception and appreciation permits the transfiguration of power and

DOI: 10.1057/9781137505903.0004

economic relations into sublimated relations based on benevolent pater-nalism, or affection, and gratitude (1998: 100–4, Verhezen 2005: 57–8).

Investigating gift-giving practices from a broad historical and philo-sophical perspective, Hénaff has efficaciously highlighted that discussing the *practice* of gift in general entails a 'serious epistemological risk' (2010b: 69) because such a practice cannot be discussed without declaring the context in which it occurs, in which it is situated. Based on his conspicu-ous analysis of many historical forms of gift-giving practices, he intro-duces three categories of gift-exchange, namely, the *ceremonial gift-giving*, the *gracious gift-giving* and the *mutual aid* or *solidarity-based gift-giving* (2010b, 2010c). According to Hénaff's interpretation, the category of the *ceremonial gift-giving*, which he derives from a different interpretation of Mauss's findings, does not pertain to the economic or moral field. Rather, it represents a tool to gain and preserve *public recognition*, namely prestige and rank; it implies *reciprocity* and it concerns relationships established between groups for the sake of establishing alliance and ensuring peace; and its lexical field is defined by the dynamic of gift/counter-gift as expressed by the Greek '*dosis/anti-dosis*' (2010b: 66–9, 2010c: 10–11). On the other hand, what Hénaff efficaciously terms *gracious gift-giving* concerns a different set of relationships which are those produced by *unilateral* gift-giving that is extended without any expectation of recip-rocation and whose purpose is not to respond to a *need*; its lexical field is defined by the *kharis* of ancient Greece, which means at the same time 'joy' and 'grace', by the Biblical *kharis* and by the Latin concept of *gratia* (2010b: 65–6, 2010c: 10–11). The category of the gracious gift-giving deserves some further clarification that can be derived from Hénaff's impressive and very precious work *The Price of Truth* (2010a).

The realm that is opened by such category, that resonates well with the common conception of the pure gift, is in fact the intricate domain where, as Hénaff emphasises, the 'visible is split from the invisible and matter from intention', where the 'internalized purpose' of the giver is claimed to constitute the 'truth' of the forms through which gifts are given (2010a: 266), where the 'moralization of the gesture of giving' seems sufficient to preserve the productiveness of the gift (2010a: 261, see 259–66). As Hénaff further highlights, reflection that focuses on 'giving for the sake of giving' emerged in ancient times as a response to the crisis of traditional gift-exchange and as a result of the intention to preserve giving, and its socially productive function, while cleansing it of its traditional forms (2010a: 260).

DOI: 10.1057/9781137505903.0004

It is in this context that giving gifts has become a *virtue* and has started to be intended as an unconditional, unilateral practice and therefore no longer primarily as a social, reciprocal one. A remarkable example of this shift is provided by the various passages of Seneca's *De beneficiis* that Hénaff quotes at length. In one of them, the logical and ethical primacy of the giver, namely of the giver's *intention*, is particularly evident:

> it is neither gold nor silver nor any of the gifts which are held to be most valuable that constitutes a benefit, but merely the *goodwill* of him who bestows it. (Seneca quoted in Hénaff 2010a: 263, emphasis added).

Another passage of *De beneficiis* (2.3–2.5, Book I) not quoted by Hénaff, reads:

> A good man never thinks about his gifts unless he is reminded by someone wishing to repay them. Otherwise the benefits are converted into loans. Treating a benefit as an expenditure is a shameful form of loan-sharking. (2.4) No matter how previous benefits have turned out, carry on bestowing them on others. They will be better off in the hands of the ungrateful who might perhaps be made grateful some day by a sense of shame, a convenient opportunity, or emulation. Do not give up. *Keep on with your task and fulfill the role of a good man.* Assist one person with wealth, someone else with credit, another with your influence, someone else with your advice, another with sensible instructions. (2.5) *Even beasts are aware of kindnesses, and no animal is so intractable that care and attention will not gentle it and produce affection towards his handler.* (Seneca 2011: 20, emphasis added).

As Hénaff points out, the absolute *position* that is attributed to the giver reflects the idea that as reciprocity is not ensured, and the only certainty is the giving subject, to give and to continue to give is a moral and *internalised* act necessary to guarantee that the community will not collapse. It is also however the expression of a long-lasting attitude as well as the initial phase of a long history and a persisting narrative, according to which the other disappears from the working of the gift and loses its autonomy and identity. The 'other' is *produced* by and *deduced* from the self (2010a: 258,263) and it is shaped by the *examples* and *values* the giver is capable of transmitting through the moral value of their gesture. In this realm, the *ethics* of giving as exemplified by Seneca's reflection will soon be superseded, as Hénaff has shown in his account, by the 'more complete and powerful symbolic system' provided by Christianity (2010a: 266). In this context, drawing from Hebrew and Greek traditions Paul will articulate a call for unconditional giving. In Pauline thought giving without reciprocation will receive its meaning only 'by taking part in the gift of Christ', in the double sense that the pure gift is the giving of 'the very person of the giver', an expression of faith and absolute trust, and that it is made possible because of the original gift from God which is 'the divine gift that is Christ himself' (2010a: 267, 268). In addition, the universal character of salvation in Christ, the Christian *kharis* will extend the realm of the pure gift beyond the limits of an ethnic group or of a material community towards the entire humankind (2010a: 268, 277). The realm opened by the gracious practice of gift has been (and still is) the field where *generosity* and *magnanimity, pure generosity devoid of calculation*, come into play as the *discrete* moral values upon which and through which social relationships are to be developed. It is in this realm that gift-giving has become (and still is) entangled with religious *charity*, with *alms, oblation, 'good deeds'.*[7] It is in this realm too that a *tension* between the *reality* and the *ideality* of the practice of gift has been introduced, as we have seen, with the effect of devaluating from an ethical point of view the *reciprocal* practices that did not comply with the *ideal.*

The category that Hénaff terms *solidarity-based gift-giving* covers giving practices that express a more social dimension and are meant to respond to *scarcity*, to help and support those who are in need. Its lexical field is that of the Aristotelian *philia* and of the Weberian 'religious ethic of brotherhood' (2010b: 66, 2010c: 10–11). This category is the realm of *compassion* and *solidarity*, it implies more an idea and an ethic of *sharing* than of *returning*, and it can be *unilateral* or *mutual* (2010c: 10–11, see 17–19). As Hénaff illustrates, Weber's concept of fraternity arises within the context of his analysis of prophetic or ascetic movements of salvation that emerged within established religions (2010a: 277). In the essay entitled *Religious Rejections of the World and Their Directions* (1920), Weber highlights how religious communities based on prophecies of salvation have extended by increasingly devaluing the exclusiveness of kinship and matrimonial relationships as the basic principle of the communal bond in favour of the bond of faith. In this way they have transferred the original principles of social and ethical conduct which informed the 'ancient economic ethic of neighbourliness', typical of every community, to the relations 'among brethren of the faith' (1946[1920]: 329). In the ethic of brotherliness so defined and developed, in this relationship of fraternity based on 'the suffering common to all believers' (1946[1920]: 330), not only is mutual aid obligatory but it also assumes a different meaning and extension to the traditional one:

DOI: 10.1057/9781137505903.0004

What had previously been the obligations of the noble and the wealthy became the fundamental imperatives of all ethically rationalized religions of the world: to aid widows and orphans in distress, to care for the sick and impoverished brother of the faith, and to give alms. [...] Externally, such commands rose to a communism of loving brethren; internally they rose to the attitude of *caritas*, love for the sufferer *per se*, for one's neighbour, for man, and finally for the enemy. [...] in direction of a universalist brotherhood, which goes beyond all barriers of societal associations, often including that of one's own faith. (1946[1920]: 329–30)

A classical theme in ancient ethical thinking (see Natali 2008) is friendship or *philia*. It occupies a central place in Aristotle's reflection so much so that he devotes two entire books of *Nicomachean Ethics* and an entire book of *Eudemian Ethics*. While his argumentations on the matter have been subject to different interpretations (see Natali 2008, Konstan 2008), the common ground is represented by the fact that for Aristotle friendship is a crucial *ethical* and *political* theme as it is the aim of politics to promote friendship amongst citizens given it encourages and ensures a respect for *justice* and is necessary for *good life* (Natali 2008: 17, Woodruff 2002: 123). In addition, according to Aristotle, friendship is not only 'the thread that knits together the social fabric' (Woodruff 2002: 123), but it is also an essential component of humanity as 'without friends, no one would choose to live' (Aristotle quoted in Woodruff 2002: 123).

Taking into account the plurality of meanings and phenomena that may figure under the heading of friendship, Aristotle thus identifies three types of friendship *between equals*, respectively revolving around *goodness*, *utility* and *pleasure*. The first constitutes the highest form of friendship for it is only in this one that good things are wished not only 'for the other for the other's sake', which is common to all forms of friendship, but also because the other is recognised as good in himself and therefore not because of other incidental causes such as his being useful or pleasant (Natali 2008: 23–4, see Konstan 2008: 210–11). It is only in the context of perfect friendship that, as Woodruff emphasises, giving and receiving are equalised without leaving space for the operation of debt, for 'calculation' and 'complaints' (2002: 123–7). As Aristotle affirms:

This kind of friendship, then, is perfect ... and in it each gets from each in all respects the same as, or something like what, he gives; which is what ought to happen between friends. (Aristotle quoted in Woodruff 2002: 123)

DOI: 10.1057/9781137505903.0004

In this context, *equality*[8] is a condition of friendship, whereas in friendship *between unequals*, which is based on superiority (father/child, husband/wife, governors/governed), *equality may be the result of friendship* (Ceron 2012: 144–5, Nepi 2006: 189). Perfect friendship is the space in which gift-giving does not translate into persistent indebtedness since it is continual, reciprocal and recognised and it creates *mutuality* (Woodruff 2002: 124). In Aristotle's perspective, the relation with the 'other', with an *equal*, a friend and not an anonymous or abstract one, is crucial for the self in order to understand and recognise himself, as the friend is 'another self' (Aristotle quoted in Woodruff 2002: 124), and it is only from this relationship that *happiness* may arise (Natali 2008: 24). More importantly, having friends is necessary in order to be able to exercise the social virtues that pertain to life in a *community*, to the life of citizens in a *polis* (Natali 2008: 24–5).

As it emerges from this short and very limited account, reflection on gift seems to be bound to movement along a spectrum of coexisting possibilities: from its purity to its intrinsically deceptive nature; from generosity and altruism to self-interest; from concern for the other to appropriation, control and manipulation of the other; from closeness to distance; from transformation to conservation of existing relationships; from reciprocal, horizontal practices, to unilateral, vertical practices; from segmented, dual reciprocity to extended, reticular mutuality; from a limited community to universal aspirations; and from theory and ideality to practice and reality. Whereas it seems quite easy to say, especially in the 'modernised' world, what a gift *is not*, it becomes very difficult to assertively articulate what a gift *is*.

The concept of gift seems in fact to convey a *pluriverse*: a pluriverse of divergent possibilities, coexisting ambiguities, undetermined interactions and multiple domains that challenges any idea of fixity, certainty and crystal clear boundaries. The gift may tell many stories and carries with it many legacies. It has a strong memory that does not keep it back from looking towards the future. Its practices are varied, variable and significantly different from each other, and the context, in its broadest, more dense and more invested sense, matters (Satlow 2013: 1). But the many questions that revolve around the gift are also 'narrative matters', for integral to the gift is the discursive production of the act of giving, of the self and of the other (Osteen 2002: 1, Derrida 1992: 10–11). The inherent difficulty with the concept of gift lies in its intrinsically elusive and opaque nature. The concept in fact signifies a relationship, a discrete

DOI: 10.1057/9781137505903.0004

relationship between a (individual or collective) *giver* and a (individual or collective) *receiver* that is created and mediated through a *thing*. As such, it is a relationship that cannot be captured by focusing on just one of its components and that opens a *situated temporal* and *practical space* that did not exist before, where no formalised conditions are laid down and no guarantees are provided (see Godbout and Caillé 1998, Godbout 2006). It is a relationship that both exposes the identity of the two sides and also produces their identification. On each side, it is fraught with potentiality, risks and aspirations, with *real* non-formalised rules, and with varied and variable *idealistic* meanings. Giving a gift means in fact to cross boundaries, to embrace the uncertain, to exceed in the etymological sense of the Latin verb *ex-cedere*: 'to surpass, to go too far' (Marramao 2011). In this sense, the concept of gift is *excessive*. It exceeds the mere reference to the *subjects* and to the *object* of the gift. It exceeds the 'modern' categories we are equipped with to understand reality. It is neglected as non-productive in relation to the 'modern' ordering of the state and the market. As their *negative* it nevertheless *positively* signals the existence of a discrete, specific relationship that traverses many domains and dimensions, particularly the 'modern' ones, whereas at the same time it cannot be reduced to any of them. That opens a *temporal* and *practical space* that is not universally the same. For this study, this is the perspective arising from the concept of gift that provides a precious hermeneutical category useful for the investigation of foreign aid.

Internationalising the gift

> *Generous persons will prosper.*
>
> (*Proverbs, 11:25*)

Along with the *doux commerce* and war, gift-giving practices have always been part of relationships between different political entities from antiquity up to the 'modernized' era, and have pervaded colonial relationships. They have always had difficulties in coexisting in both the domain of external relations and the domestic one, with the vicious, disruptive operation and logic of bribery phenomena[9] (Verhezen 2005, Liebersohn 2011, Satlow 2013). Assuming that the 'pretense and elaborate machinery of foreign aid for economic development' would be nothing more than the substitute for 'the traditional businesslike transmission of

DOI: 10.1057/9781137505903.0004

bribes' (1962: 302), in his pioneering dissection of foreign aid endeavour Morgenthau highlighted that whereas:

> bribes proffered by one government to another for political advantage were until the beginning of the nineteenth century an integral part of the armory of diplomacy [...] these bribes [*meaning foreign aid*] are a less effective means for the purpose of purchasing political favors than were the traditional ones. (Morgenthau 1962: 302)

On the opposite side, as we have seen, Mauss proposed a *total* revaluation, particularly but not solely in moral terms, of gift-giving practices to be intended as a *rational* (even though imbued with *irrational* forms and contents) and *public* tool to *progress*. A tool to enable one to build alliances and to ensure peace, or at least to control conflict both in the domestic domain and also in external relations, between societies and groups that otherwise would be poised against each other in a Hobbesian-like situation of continuous threat of war (see Sahlins 1968, 1972, Hénaff 2010b). Turning the spotlight onto the diverse writings Mauss consecrated in 1923 and 1924 (within the context of his participation in socialist and solidarist movements) to the German war reparations and debt crisis, Mallard (2010) recently put forward an interesting, *à la Skinner* investigation of the context and the intention behind the writing of *The Gift*. In so doing, he has thus opened yet another frontier for the rereading and possible international projection of Maussian theory (see also Liebersohn 2011: 139–65).

From a contextual analysis point of view, Mallard submits that one of the intentions of Mauss was to provide *legal* grounds, particularly through the investigation of ancient Germanic law, for his political claims that France and its Allies should make a *gift* to Germany by writing off a large amount of its reparation debt and by granting to the Germans an *adequately long* moratorium on payments that would allow them to reorganise their economic and financial system. In this light, *The Gift* would thus also serve to demonstrate that gift-exchange practices, being part of all legal traditions (the European one included) and being capable of constructing a *legal rule* (what Mauss termed in French *règle de droit*), could through their own rules still effectively produce *duties*. Germany, therefore, as the receiver of a gift, provided that it was not irrationally forced to respond with a simultaneous counter-gift, would understand the rules of gift-exchange and pay back reparations (2010: 24–37). By further expanding, Mallard argues that *The Gift* provided

DOI: 10.1057/9781137505903.0004

'a normative model of international law' in that it explained how the exchange-through-gift could serve the cause of international peace and cooperation (2010: 43, 36–7).

A fair number of varied and valuable studies have further elaborated on the internationalisation of gift-giving practices by drawing on Mauss's theory to inspect the operations, intentions and narratives of foreign aid. While some have done so from a perspective that predominantly focuses on global dynamics (Hattori 2001, 2003, Latouche 2005, Kapoor 2008, Kowalski 2011), others have adopted a more geographically situated and/ or ethnographical point of view (Aaltola 1999, Silk 2004, Eyben 2005, 2006, Eyben and Léon 2005, Eyben et al. 2007, Silva 2008); and yet others have further expanded the scope by using the theory of gift to assess the impact of foreign aid upon social relations in recipient communities (Ivarsson Holgersson 2013), or to investigate South–South (Mawdsley 2012) or East–South (Gray 2011) foreign aid practices.

Within the context of this limited but promising and burgeoning field of investigation, this study positions itself within the 'first group', but with some particularities. Whereas the adoption of the concept of gift as a precious hermeneutical tool is the common ground, within the scope of this analysis the concept of gift is however intended only as the concept that can help to shed light on a discrete, specific set of relationships. This means that whereas such an approach is surely informed by Mauss and other scholars' contribution concerning the various dimensions the gift intersects and activates in its 'movement', and through its main logic, it does not revolve around the sole Maussian conceptualisation of gift, nor does it assume any other *a priori* dense conceptualisation, model or ideal type. In this context, the concept of the gift is in fact intended as the notion that allows the correct conceptualisation of foreign aid and prevents its forced and incorrect reduction, or equation, with contiguous categories which are however different such as economic exchange or redistribution (see Hattori 2001: 635–9). Despite its vague official definition (see Hynes and Scott 2013), it seems quite evident that, from a conceptual point of view, foreign aid, also frequently called 'development assistance', 'development coopera-tion' or 'development aid', is an international and composite gift. It is the *voluntary* extension of a varied and variable set of resources such as physical goods, skills and technical know-how, financial grants or loans at concessional rates, from a collective subject (the donor) to another (the recipient one or a group of them). Affirming that foreign aid is a gift does not imply however that it constitutes the simple reflection or reproduction of an already known form or model of gift, nor that the set of practices that originate from it are easily predictable, or even that they are the simple international replication of the ones whose logic has been scrutinised and detected in the gift literature. It neither implies that the concept of gift provides all answers or that it can be used to analyse the whole set of practices and their multiple and varied dimensions and actors. On the contrary, in order to avoid the epistemological trap of assuming that gift and gift-giving practices are everywhere and at any moment the same, the analytical attention should focus on the mosaic of relationships that is *positively* produced, informed and kept in motion by it. Furthermore, additional attention needs to be given to the careful consideration of the peculiar, fragmented and complex *context* within which foreign aid practices unfold and which they contribute to reshape. If, as I assume with other scholars, foreign aid is gift, it is so in a new, specific and not already encountered way. Therefore, its *political practical* productivity cannot be *a priori* reduced to any previous model but deserves to be addressed anew.

The crucial point of departure for this investigation is represented by the Foucauldian notions of 'government' and 'governmentality', which in fact have been used by many authors to investigate and explain in various ways the operation and effects of foreign aid practices (see Ferguson 1994, Duffield 2001a, 2002, Ferguson and Gupta 2002, Mosse 2005a, Gould 2005, Anders 2005, Lie 2005, Escobar 2012).[10] In the context of this productive line of thought, this study attempts to analyse foreign aid by drawing on Dean's elaboration of the *analytics of government*. Dean defines his rich, convincing and intriguing perspective by placing the concepts of 'government' and 'governmentality' within the context of Foucault's broader reflection on relations of power and by drawing upon a wide range of other critical resources provided by the same Foucault, Deleuze and many other authors (2010, see also Lemke 2007). Dean expands the Foucauldian definition of 'government' as the 'conduct of conduct' by defining it as:

> *any more or less calculated and rational activity, undertaken by a multiplicity of authorities and agencies, employing a variety of techniques and forms of knowledge, that seeks to shape conduct by working through the desires, aspirations, interest and beliefs of various actors, for definite but shifting ends and with a diverse set of relatively unpredictable consequences, effects and outcomes.* (2010: 18)

DOI: 10.1057/9781137505903.0004

In this context, 'governing' is to be intended as an *art* that requires 'craft, imagination, shrewd fashioning, the use of tacit skills and practical know-how'. An art that requires various forms of thought 'about the nature of rule and knowledge of who and what are to be governed'; that involves the use of particular techniques, skills and practical know-how to achieve its aims; that establishes 'identities for the governed and the governors'; and that 'involves a more or less subtle direction of the conduct of the governed' (2010: 28). The object of an analytics of government is thus not the 'simple empirical activity of governing' or the 'actual relations of authority and domination', but the '*art of government*'. An analytics of government is, as Dean further explains, a study of 'the organized practices through which we are governed and we govern ourselves' – a study of what he calls *regimes of practices* or *regimes of government* (2010: 28). According to Dean, such regimes of practices can be identified whenever:

> there exists a relatively stable field of correlation of visibilities, mentalities, technologies and agencies, such that they constitute a kind of taken-for-granted point of reference for any form of problematization. (2010: 37)

In relation to such evidence, the aim of an analytics of government is then to take seriously the *singularity* of each particular regime of practices through an analytics that:

> seeks to identify the *emergence* of that regime, examine the multiple *sources* of the elements that constitute it, and follow the diverse *processes* and *relations* by which these elements are assembled into relatively stable *forms of organization* and *institutional practice*. It examines how such regime gives rise to and depends upon particular forms of *knowledge* and how, as a consequence of this, it becomes the target of various *programmes* of reform and change. It considers how this regime has a *technical* or technological dimension and analyses the characteristic techniques, instrumentalities and mechanisms through which such practices operate, by which they attempt to realize their goals, and through which they have a range of effects. (Dean 2010: 31, emphasis added)

As Dean illustrates, such a perspective rejects any *a priori* and taken-for-granted distribution, division and identification of power and authority. It focuses on the ways in which governmental practices include practices of self-government; 'form and increase the capabilities and autonomy of individuals and collectives'; and in doing so also lead to an 'intensification of power relations' (Dean 2010: 49 quoting Foucault). It assumes that government is conducted in '*plural*' as there is a 'plurality of governing

DOI: 10.1057/9781137505903.0004

agencies and authorities, of aspects of behaviour to be governed, of norms invoked, of purposes sought, and of effects, outcomes and consequences' (2010: 18, emphasis added). It focuses attention on the ways in which the forms of knowledge that are produced by a regime of practices, and that in turn shape and reshape it, are to be investigated in the explicit *programmes*, theories and policies where they accumulate. On the other hand, this perspective draws attention to the need to complement this investigation with the analysis of the intrinsic logic of such a regime: of its 'non-subjective intentionality that can be constructed through analysis' (2010: 32); of its strategy intended as 'the medium in which government exists rather than its instrument' (2010: 269). A strategy or logic that can be captured by identifying '"inconvenient facts"' such as the disjunction between the explicit, stated aims of particular programmes and other programmatic rationalities and their diverse effects (2010: 52). In the rich description of his approach, Dean singles out the four main dimensions through which the object 'assemblage' or 'regime of practices' can be searched through. Four dimensions that in Dean's perspective are to be thought as always simultaneously present and mutually involving within each regime of practices, with each moving along its own trajectory, not reducible to each other (2010: 33). These dimensions are:

1 characteristic forms of *visibility*, ways of seeing and perceiving
2 distinctive ways of *thinking and questioning*, relying on definite vocabularies and procedures for the production of truth (e.g. those derived from the social, human and behavioural sciences)
3 specific ways of *acting, intervening and directing*, made up of particular types of practical rationality ('expertise' and 'know-how'), and relying upon definite mechanisms, techniques and technologies
4 characteristic ways of *forming subjects*, selves, persons, actors or agents
   (2010: 33, emphasis added).

The next chapter is an attempt to apply the richness of the insights provided by the analytical perspective elaborated by Dean to analyse foreign aid practices as constituting a peculiar regime of practices of government. The following chapter will complement the analysis with the investigation of the ways in which the notion of sovereignty together with its shifting conceptions form part of the foreign aid regime governmental rationality.[11]

Notes

1   A partial sampling of recent historiographical investigations of the practice of gift in different geographical contexts and historical periods includes Davis (2000), Athané (2008), Zionkowski and Klekar (2009), Satlow (2013), Carlà and Gori (2014).

2   It is worth noticing that there are at least two main tendencies in the broad field of the historiography of the gift. First is the evolutionary one, which includes under some perspectives Mauss himself, Polanyi and Duby amongst others. For them the gift is a predecessor of state redistribution and market exchange that has maintained only a residual role in modern societies. Within this school of thought, extremely varied are however the hypotheses regarding when/where to place the 'turning point'. The second broad trend, which includes again Mauss, Caillé and the so-called third Paradigm school, as well as other members of the *Revue du M.A.U.S.S.* *(Mouvement anti-utilitariste dans le sciences sociales)*, is based on the assumption that the gift would constitute a 'natural constant' throughout history and in every society (Athané 2008: 317–replace with: 19, Carlà and Gori 2014: 13–16).

3   Mauss used the French term *prestation*. The translation with the term *services* is not completely satisfying, and for instance Cunnison's translation of *The Gift* (1966), which is highly contested for many other inaccuracies, maintains the French word without attempting any translation of it. Within the compass of this study the English translation with 'services' is however maintained for the sake of consistency with the translation by Halls which is the one that is used in this context.

4   The dangerous nature of the gift is constitutive of German costume and is reflected by the ancient German word 'Gift' that means both 'gift' and 'poison' (Mauss 2002[1923–4]:81, see also Benveniste 1969).

5   According to the Oxford English Dictionary, a gift is 'something, the possession of which is transferred to another without the expectation or receipt of an equivalent; a donation, present'.

6   According to Bourdieu the 'symbolic capital' is correlated with any other type of capital as it is 'any property (any form of capital whether physical, economic, cultural or social) when it is perceived by social agents endowed with categories of perception which cause them to know it and to recognize it, to give it value' (1998: 47, see 47–52).

7   For the different interpretation of the gift elaborated within the context of the Protestant doctrine of predestination, see Hénaff (2010a: 268–76).

8   In Aristotle's reflection the condition of equality concerns only the citizens as a *polis* is organised around varied forms of inequalities, the most paradigmatic of which is the difference between citizens and slaves (see Nepi 2006:188).

DOI: 10.1057/9781137505903.0004

9 For a very rich and interesting investigation of the complex relations between gifts and bribes, see Verhezen (2005).

10 Whereas some of these authors tend to analyse aid as a form of liberal global *governance*, within the context of this study the term 'government' is preferred for many of the reasons that are carefully expressed by Lemke (2007) and Dean (2007: 139–46). Drawing on Foucault's notion of governmentality, in recent times some scholars have used the concept of 'developmentality', see Lie (2005) and Mawulo-Yevugah (2011). On the concept of governmentality, see Dean (2010: 16–30).

11 Following Dean the rationality of government can be defined as: 'any relatively systematic way of thinking about government. This can include the form of representation for the field to be governed, the agencies to be considered and enrolled in governing, the techniques to be employed, and the ends to be achieved. Rationalities of government can be theoretical knowledges, particular programmes, forms of practical know-how, or strategies' (2010: 268).

DOI: 10.1057/9781137505903.0004

2
The Foreign Aid Regime

Abstract: *Foreign aid practices constitute a particular regime of government: with its own truth, discourse and knowledge, its own explicit aims and programme; and its own intrinsic logic and strategy. Adopting a historical perspective, this chapter illustrates how the foreign aid regime has emerged after the end of the Second World War as a regime of government of North–South relations, and how it has increasingly expanded to a regime of government of South countries and selected groups of populations within and across them. Although Furia acknowledges that foreign aid practices carry a function in the conservation of economic and geopolitical/strategic power relations, she argues the reason for doing so lies in their peculiar and continuous potential for transformation of the same relations.*

Keywords: accountability/trust in donor/recipient relationship; development truth/knowledge/discourse; human/global security; North–South relations

Furia, Annalisa. *The Foreign Aid Regime: Gift-Giving, States and Global Dis/Order.* Basingstoke: Palgrave Macmillan, 2015. DOI: 10.1057/9781137505903.0005.

Whereas the exchange of gifts between different political entities has deeper historical roots, the emergence of foreign aid as a regime of practices that possesses its 'own specific regularities, logic, strategy, self-evidence and "reason"' (Foucault quoted in Dean 2010: 3), dates back to the post-Second World War period. An author who has thoroughly engaged with the analysis of the ways in which the practice of gift relates to power, economic hierarchies and domination dynamics is Bourdieu (see Chapter 1). Whereas Bourdieu's analysis is crucial in capturing many features of foreign aid practices as gift-giving practices, it is not enough. As highlighted in the previous chapter, the ways in which the foreign aid regime operates needs to be specifically addressed by taking into account the following: the historical conditions of its emergence and its peculiar spatial dimension(s); the ever-evolving truth, discourse and forms of knowledge that inform foreign aid practices and that are continuously reshaped by them; the foreign aid regime's specific techniques, language and instruments; the ways in which the identities of the actors involved in the foreign aid regime are formed; and the specific powers that are allocated to them.

Following the methodological approach described in the previous chapter, this chapter attempts to focus attention on the specificities of this regime of practices. This is done by scrutinising in the first section the historical context in which the foreign aid regime emerged. The second section delineates the ways in which development has provided the foreign aid regime with a set of governmental programmes, strategies and technologies. In the third section, attention is given to the perspectives according to which the various actors are constructed and made visible in the foreign aid regime. Particular attention is given to the technical tools by means of which *trust* and *accountability* are formed and 'distributed' in the foreign aid regime. Finally, the fourth section investigates the intrinsic logic upon which the foreign aid regime operates and focuses attention to the ways in which the notions of *debt* and *identity*, critical to any gift-giving relationship, are peculiarly re-shaped. For the sake of clarity, all aspects addressed are analysed separately, although they are closely interlinked.

The new name of peace

Tempora mutantur et nos mutamur in illis.

DOI: 10.1057/9781137505903.0005

The closer predecessors of the multiple activities that figure in the contemporary foreign aid regime can be identified in the assistance and technical plans of the late colonial imperialist governments and in governmental and non-governmental relief and humanitarian interventions of the end of the nineteenth century. They can also be found in the League of Nations's pioneering attempt to internationalise technical support measures.

Towards the end of the nineteenth century, colonial powers had started to extend assistance and promote the development, namely the '*mise en valeur*' (turning into account), of their colonial possessions through the designing and application of various scientific and technological programmes. These programmes would allow properly trained colonial officers to modernise strategic economic and social sectors of colonial territories (for instance, extraction of raw materials, agriculture, health care, education), as well as colonised populations (Rist 2008, Unger 2010, Frey and Kunkel 2011).

Outside the context of colonial domination, in 1812, the United States adopted the first recorded governmental act of foreign relief called the 'Act for the Relief of Citizens of Venezuela'. It was aimed at supporting Venezuelan citizens after the earthquake that had affected the country in March of that same year. Over the years, the United States increasingly facilitated private solidarity efforts. They provided transportation for private donations intended to assist foreign people and in some cases they directly funded foreign governments to assist people affected by natural disasters. On a different note, in 1896, the United States promoted the external transfer of domestic food surplus 'for market development'. This transfer would regularly continue after the First World War (not only in emergency situations), particularly since the adoption of the 1933 Agricultural Adjustment Act. This Act envisaged the establishment of the Commodity Credit Corporation with the aim amongst others, of developing new foreign markets for the agricultural products of the United States (Hjertholm and White 2000: 4–5, National Research Council et al. 1978: 7–9).

Around the same time, aid campaigns and relief initiatives were increasingly carried out by different agencies, such as the Red Cross (founded in 1863) and other, religious and international organisations. The most famous example in this field is represented by the China International Famine Relief Commission, established in China by foreign residents in the aftermath of a massive famine in 1921. This Commission

DOI: 10.1057/9781137505903.0005

promoted agrarian and education reform projects in order to prevent further famines and promote economic development.

In this composite context, it was particularly the League of Nations's efforts that expressed a collective, institutional and somehow 'harmonised' action on the matter. Action that would contribute in paving the way for the post-Second World War enterprise. The League of Nations also experienced most of the dynamics that will be, irremediably, part of the post-war endeavour as well. One of the most evident is the attempt to embody internationalist aspirations, and to supervise and guide a common 'determined effort to organize peace' (League of Nations quoted in Zanasi 2007: 149) in a context that was dominated, and would be for a long time dominated, by colonial thinking and colonial powers' concrete interests and persisting logic. Whereas the League's mission was to promote 'international co-operation' and 'peace and security' amongst nations and to adhere to the principles of national sovereignty and equality among nations (Zanasi 2007: 146), the conflict about the destiny (attribution) of the territorial possessions of the empires defeated in the First World War made evident the need to reach a compromise between internationalist and anti-colonial criticisms and the very vivid colonial interests (Zanasi 2007: 146–8, Rist 2008: 59–60). The mandates system, established by Article 22 of the Covenant of the League of Nations, cemented the compromise that was reached. Within this system, the former colonies and territories of the defeated empires were entrusted to 'advanced nations' (mostly France and Britain) that, taking into account *the stage of development of the people*, were considered the best candidates to exercise a 'tutelage' over them (League of Nations 1919: art. 22, paras 2 and 3, emphasis added). As 'mandatories' of the League, the entrusted powers would allow international monitoring of their own administration by reporting every year to the Permanent Mandates Commission (art. 22, paras 7–9). The attempt to move beyond the traditional colonial system fell far short of any substantial innovation as most of the mandatory powers were members of the Mandates Commission and the Commission itself had no other power than that of formulating recommendations. In spite of this the notion of international perspective started to work its way up to the redefinition of the space where states were to oppose each other and to interact (Rist 2008: 63, 66–7). The mandates system was a genuine expression of the colonialist civilising mission, with its 'pedagogical' and 'educational' aims, age-old evolutionary narrative, composite modernising ambitions and pervasive paternalism. However,

DOI: 10.1057/9781137505903.0005

it also embodied an attempt to 'internationalize the civilizing mission' by suggesting that the 'well-being and development' of the least advanced countries formed a 'sacred trust of civilisation' whose fulfilment could no longer fall solely on individual, single states' responsibility but had to constitute a kind of collective duty (League of Nations 1919: art. 22, para. 1, Zanasi 2007: 144–8). As Rist effectively highlights, the international-ism of the League of Nations reveals the emergence of a *'political and symbolic space'* where states 'discussed together even as they clashed on the ground', where 'at least they agreed to recognize one another's right to profit from their conquests'. This new international space comple-mented the national one. Whereas the national 'grabbed hold of places and living people', the international 'exerted its sway over minds in the name of universalism and humanity' (2008: 67). The League attempted to apply the same perspective to its 'technical' interventions. Through its non-political organisations, it tried to coordinate member states' finan-cial and technical aid with the aim, in the first phase, to assist countries affected by the First World War and to address war related plights, such as that of war refugees, or other humanitarian concerns (Zanasi 2007: 149). It was at a later stage that the League of Nations increasingly began to make reference to the need to stabilise transnational economic, finan-cial and social trends in order to secure peace, stability and growth in an interdependent world. In a bid to 'prevent' and 'cure' at the international level the disruptive effects of poverty, health diseases and labour issues, the League subsequently extended its intervention to support the 'least advanced' countries, including former colonies or semi-colonies such as China (2007: 148–50). Anticipating the main features of its post-Second World War descendant, the League's approach, based on the 'traditional' evolutionary narrative according to which all states would pass through the same stages of evolution, viewed all the least advanced countries as belonging to a supposed, uniform 'third phase of development' (2007: 148). It built on the need to promote 'intellectual cooperation' by diffus-ing the values of modernisation and civilisation (2007:148). It presented itself through the reassuring faces of 'international experts' who were supposed to work no longer for the interests of a single metropole, but for the 'bettering of humanity' and particularly for curing 'economic and financial *malaise* prevalent throughout the world' (League of Nations quoted in Zanasi 2007: 144, 150). In contrast to colonial interventions, the League's approach implied the recruitment of experts based on sectoral technical expertise more than regional experience or knowledge of local language, culture and costume. The result was an implementation of standardised, difference blind and poorly geographically specialised technical and financial assistance plans (Zanasi 2007: 144, see also Kothari 2005: 57–61).

As shown by the League's internationalising efforts, after the First World War and in a more compelling way after the Second World War, the *interdependence* of nations had come to constitute the space to be made governable, the *de facto* condition made visible by the world wars themselves to be made 'thinkable', 'knowable' and 'actionable' (Dean 2010: 238). It is in this context that the practice of voluntary giving among nations has been reshaped, extended and progressively valued by Western states as a tool to cope, individually and through a communal effort, with the problems raised by the new international setting. The first evidence of the formation of a new international governmental practice emerged in the actions and strategy designed by the new political and economic power consecrated by the end of the second World, that is the United States. In May 1947, the United States Congress approved the Greek–Turkish Aid Act to support Greek and Turkish efforts to resist communist forces by sending economic and military aid; and in April 1948, the Marshall Plan, proposed in 1947, was adopted to give monetary support to European countries for the rebuilding of their economies and to prevent the spread of communism to Western Europe. Although initially engaged in responding to the political and economic effects of the war in Europe, the major powers then increasingly started to extend their attention to the conditions of the South (see Rist 2008: 70, footnote 1). A preliminary example of this orientation is represented by the adoption of two resolutions – respectively entitled 'Economic Development of Underdeveloped Countries' (198 – III) and 'Technical Assistance for Economic Development' (200 – III) – that were adopted on 4 December 1948 by the General Assembly of the United Nations on the basis of the consideration that:

> the low standards of living existing in Member States have bad economic and social effects in the countries directly concerned and *on the world as a whole*, and create conditions of *instability* which are *prejudicial to the maintenance of peaceful and friendly relations among nations* and to the development of conditions of economic and social progress. (UN 1948a: para. 1, emphasis added)

In its resolutions, the General Assembly recommended that the Economic and Social Council and the specialised agencies should

DOI: 10.1057/9781137505903.0005

give 'further and urgent consideration to the whole problem of the economic development of *under-developed* countries in *all* its aspects'. It endorsed the hope, expressed by the Economic and Social Council, that the International Bank for Reconstruction and Development (better known as the World Bank) would take immediate steps to facilitate the realisation of '*development loans*' (UN 1948a: paras 3 and 4, emphasis added). A crucial turning point in the formative phase of the foreign aid regime of practices would be however represented a year later by the explicit, public formulation of its programme. This programme was to be provided by President Truman's famous inaugural address known as the 'Four-Point speech'. In his speech, which crystallised the most critical characteristics of the foreign aid mission that all Western states were summoned to embark upon, President Truman reaffirmed the casual relationship amongst economic growth, stability and peace upon which the League of Nations had based its efforts. What was really new in Truman's account was the fact that such a correlation was officially named as *development*.

After the 'unprecedented and brutal attacks on the rights of man', Truman asserted, all men had 'to learn to live together in peace and harmony' (Truman 1949a: 4). Although the future was burdened with 'grave uncertainty' and 'composed almost equally of great hopes and great fears', it offered at least a certainty which was that it was possible to 'look at the United States as never before for good will, strength, and wise leadership' (1949a: 5). It was the United States that, having already defeated the *past*,[1] was called to be responsible of setting the pace of the future. As Truman proudly said: 'The initiative is ours' (1949a: 30). The United States would therefore support the enhancement of military cooperation and collective defense in the North Atlantic area by means of the North Atlantic Treaty; it would confirm its support for the United Nations and it would keep sustaining programmes for world economic recovery, first of all the European reconstruction by means of the Marshall Plan (1949a: 33–43).

In order to build, in cooperation with the United Nations and other 'like-minded nations', 'an even stronger structure of international order and justice' (1949a: 31), those three lines of action were to be complemented by the commitment to engage in a fourth one:

> Fourth, we must embark on a bold new program for making the benefits of our scientific advances and industrial progress available for the improvement and growth of underdeveloped areas. [...]

DOI: 10.1057/9781137505903.0005

I believe that we should make available to peace-loving peoples the benefits of our store of technical knowledge in order to help them realize their aspirations for a better life. And, in cooperation with other nations, we should foster capital investment in areas needing development.

Our aim should be to help the free peoples of the world, through their own efforts, to produce more food, more clothing, more materials for housing, and more mechanical power to lighten their burden.

[...] This should be a cooperative enterprise in which all nations work together through the United Nations and its specialized agencies wherever practicable. It must be a worldwide effort for the achievement of peace, plenty, and freedom. [...]

Such new economic developments must be devised and controlled to benefit the peoples of the areas in which they are established. [...]

The old imperialism – exploitation for foreign profit – has no place in our plans. What we envisage is a program of development based on the concepts of democratic fair-dealing. [...]

Only by helping the least fortunate of its members to help themselves can the human family achieve the decent, satisfying life that is the right of all people. (Truman 1949a: 44, 48–50, 52–3, 56)

In Truman's foundational, 'religious-like' speech (see Rist 2008: 77), the concept and practice of development lost its colonial mark and could advance in the path traced by the League of Nations by becoming the new collective mission of nation–states, that were all to be recognised as members of the same, universal 'human family'. From a *tool* to make occupied territories profitable, development thus became the common *objective* of all 'free' and 'peace-loving' peoples of the world (see Unger 2010). Development became a humanitarian duty, a new, owed 'sacred trust' in response to the condition of passivity, despair and suffering that united all underdeveloped peoples:

More than half the people of the world are living in conditions approaching *misery*. Their food is inadequate. They are *victims* of disease. [...]

For the first time in history, humanity possesses the knowledge and the skill to relieve the *suffering* of these people. (Truman 1949a: 45–6, emphasis added)

Development was thus presented as something *new*, a call to leave the past behind ('old imperialism', 'exploitation') and to boldly move towards a new era, towards the *future* ('for the first time in history'). Along with successfully proposing a clear conceptualisation of the relationship

DOI: 10.1057/9781137505903.0005

between the past and the future, the concept of development also shaped the space of action of foreign aid practices by providing new lenses through which the world and its actors could be viewed. In the first instance, in the development space there was no place for communism – a 'false philosophy' that is the opposite of democracy. Secondly, the space opened by development allowed the maintenance of hierarchical distinctions amongst states to be maintained, while at the same time creating a new, profoundly different, perception.

As highlighted by Rist, in Western Enlightenment the age-old idea of development had been formulated in terms of a *philosophy of history*, or in other words in terms of a 'natural history of humanity'. In this view, progress or development (expansion of knowledge and wealth) had affirmed itself as a *necessity* and as a *natural* principle inscribed in human nature (Rist 2008: 39–40).[2] By the nineteenth century, social evolutionism had further 'refined' the evolutionary paradigm by ensuring that scientific value and acceptance were attributed to the notion of development as a one-way street for all 'civilisations'. In the new post-Second World War setting formally based on the 'sovereign equality of all its members' (art. 2, para. 1 of the Charter of the United Nations), the reproduction of a simplified version of the 'scientific' evolutionary scheme (underdevelopment/development) allowed to present the *diversity* of states, not in terms of a radical 'otherness' or subordination, but in terms of a variation, of a distance (underdevelopment) from something that was assumed to be *identical* and *natural* for all the members of 'human family' (development).[3] In a world still composed of *unequal* colonies and of *unequal* territories placed under the United Nations international trusteeship system, which had replaced the mandates system, development offered a powerful, *inclusive* and future oriented perspective to deal with states' *inequality*. It was a tool by which inequality could be maintained through, amongst other ways, stigmatisation, while itself offering a solution. In this sense, the explanation put forward for diversity/inequality and for hierarchical distinctions amongst states was simultaneously and selectively: *ahistorical/historical* (underdevelopment is a state of affairs due to a country's primitiveness and not the result of the past or current conditions of domination and exploitation); properly *progressive, evolutionary* (it can be solved by moving up on the ladder of development); and rigorously *technical* (it is not a political or geopolitical

DOI: 10.1057/9781137505903.0005

problem but a matter of adequate technical, scientific knowledge and economic instruments):

> Their economic life is primitive and stagnant. [...]
>
> With the cooperation of business, private capital, agriculture, and labor in this country, this program can greatly increase the industrial activity in other nations and can raise substantially their standards of living. [...]
>
> Greater production is the key to prosperity and peace. And the key to greater production is a wider and more vigorous application of modern scientific and technical knowledge. (Truman 1949a: 45, 51, 55)

It is the fact that underdeveloped countries still live in the *past* that hinders development, and not the common *past* or the 'effects of conquest, colonization, the slave trade [...] and so on' (Rist 2008: 74). Similarly, the alleged root causes of underdevelopment are constructed *as detached from interdependence* and as intrinsic to the state in question, as derived from its domestic limitations and disadvantages:

> Their poverty is a *handicap* and a *threat* both to them and to more prosperous areas. (Truman 1949a: 45, emphasis added)

Not only were developed states not to be held responsible for other states' underdevelopment, but they were also those who were willing to provide the *solution* to the threat posed by underdevelopment. Disposing of 'imponderable resources in technical knowledge', Western states were the *natural* leaders in the development world (Truman 1949a: 47). Development being not only a common destiny but also 'a single road', Western states who had already advanced along the way were *naturally* required to continue to demonstrate what development was, show the path ahead and the instruments that had to be used. More crucially, they were willing to continue to do so not as colonisers or formal rulers but voluntarily as *generous*, donor countries; and no longer through forms of domination but through *help* and *assistance*.

In this new space of visibility, thought and action, Western foreign aid practices could no longer be suspected of belonging to, and of perpetuating, colonial development experience and relations. They could not, either, remain episodical and voluntary acts aimed at gaining political alliance and economical favour, at establishing or maintaining friendly relationships or at assisting countries affected by famine, wars and natural disasters. By being associated with the aim of *development*, which was not simply a truly modern, progressive concept, but also profoundly

DOI: 10.1057/9781137505903.0005

humanitarian, ethical, publicly appreciable and properly international in scope, Western foreign aid practices would become the tool to promote development. As highlighted by Rist, Point Four's programme put forward '*a new way of conceiving international relations*' (2008: 72). By constructing development as the solution to all ills, or better '*the only possible one*' (2008: 76), it made North–South relations governable in the name of the varied goals, ambitions and programmes of development. It transformed foreign aid practices into a needed form of interference, a *generous, morally valuable* one. It provided foreign aid practices not only with a 'good', common and ever shifting objective, but also with a vocabulary and narrative, a scientific apparatus of knowledge, techniques, specialised institutions and skilled experts, and a set of undisputable values and aspirations. Since the very first phase, development has thus represented, and still is, a new, crucial form of international governmental rationality which has sought to drastically reinvent and transform foreign aid practices, and which has been continuously reshaped and reinvented by them.

Development can be developed

> *Gutta cavat lapidem,*
> *non vi sed saepe cadendo.*

The analysis of the short, rich and vastly scrutinised history of the shifting contents that have variously substantiated the post-Second World War *truth* of development shows that that of development has constituted, and still constitutes, a particularly persuasive system of *truth(s)*, *knowledge(s)* and *discourse(s)*. As Esteva puts it: development 'occupies the centre of an incredibly powerful semantic constellation. There is nothing in modern mentality comparable to it as force guiding thought and behavior' (Esteva quoted in McVety 2008: 371–2). Such a constellation has changed and grown over the years, absorbing the new ideas, contents and principles as well as the new *theories* and *strategies* that were put forward with the aim of clarifying its proper aims, reforming its approach or improving its operations. The development constellation has constituted a flexible, accumulative and extremely 'resistant' theoretical and discursive framework in which ideas have tended to evolve but very rarely have completely vanished; in which '*normative*' theories

DOI: 10.1057/9781137505903.0005

have always coexisted with '*positive*' ones, as well as '*holistic*' theories with '*partial*' (mainly economic) ones (Potter 2008: 68–9). Whereas, as we will very shortly see, some theories and strategies may have prevailed at a particular moment, what makes the 'development constellation' still so powerful is that, on the one hand, an approach or notion discarded in some quarters (for instance in common opinion or public debate) may still retain currency in other ones (for instance at the level of implementation) (Potter 2008). On the other hand, the system of knowledge of development is grounded on *universal* principles and *predictive* models that create the epistemological conditions which allow attention to be drawn away from national/contextual differences, practical contingencies and contradictions, and alternative truths (Mosse 2005a: 6). As Mosse emphasises, development is constituted as:

> an *interpretive* order that conceals the complex politics and passions of practice, while being powerful enough (that is, in allocating both resources and legitimacy, and providing the frameworks that judge performance) to ensure that diverse events, ambitions and political exigencies *are* translated into a singular global logic. (Mosse 2005a: 24)

In this way, development is produced as a flexible and always reformed (and reformable) system of universal *truth(s)*, *knowledge(s)* and *discourse(s)*. A system that, in spite of fragmentation and multiplicity, is constantly reproduced as a *harmonic*, *unified* system. A system in which 'getting theory right' is constructed as the key to address and redress *practice* (Mosse 2005b: 1) and in which the orientation is always 'future positive' (2005b: 1 quoting Edwards). The intent to 'get theory right' and to constantly look towards the future has thus nurtured the production of an enormous amount of broad theories, middle-range strategies, official policies, statements, procedures and principles, revision and reform programmes and approaches by governments, international institutions and organisations, scholars, experts and practitioners, research centres, think-tanks and civil society organisations.

In a very broad outline, which will highlight only general trends,[4] the first major theoretical source for the development strategy and discourse was provided in the 1950s by modernisation theory. This theory, which although very much criticised is still substantially influential, responded to the problems of underdevelopment by starting from the analysis of the conditions that had allowed the development of 'modern' countries in order to identify why and in which sectors underdeveloped countries

DOI: 10.1057/9781137505903.0005

had failed to achieve such conditions. Modernisation theorists provided varying answers to such a question, which ranged from economic reasons (shortage of capital, low saving rate), to sociological and political ones (these included a lack of capitalist values and entrepreneurial spirit, and a lack of liberal democracy institutions) (Rapley 2002: 15). Their common assumption, epitomised by Rostow's *The Stages of Economic Growth* (1958), was in line with traditional evolutionism: underdevelopment was an initial phase or stage of the common, linear evolutionary path through which all states would move towards development. The nub of modernisation theories was thus based on the traditional view according to which Western states provide a 'massive demonstration' of the common, natural evolutionary path, and thus '*modernization is only a form of Westernization*' (Rist 2008: 102); Western states' knowledge, models and values offer the paradigm to be followed to promote *economic growth*, that is equated to development; and Western states' aid is necessary because it can help underdeveloped countries caught in 'poverty traps' to close their 'financing gap' thus providing a very much needed 'big push' in terms of investment and capital – according to Rosenstein-Rodan's (1943) famous paradigm – that would lead to a 'takeoff' (one of Rostow's stages of growth) into self-sustained growth (Easterly 2005: 1–5, see Abuzeid 2009).

Modernisation theories sourced their major technical tools and recipes from the neoclassical economic paradigm that focused on the vital role of *technological change* and *rationalisation* to raise productivity, and of *free trade* and *market* to maximise efficiency (Binns 2008: 82). They also abundantly sourced from what was called the 'behavioural revolution'. This revolution, which started in the United States around the late 1940s, constituted a shift in focus in social sciences methodology away from the normative study of institutions and constitutions. The new focus instead was the scientific investigation of society based on observation, comparison and classification of human behaviour 'in the hope of making general inferences about it' (Rapley 2002: 15). In such an epistemological context, the search for generalisable principles, together with *modelling* techniques, *standardisation* and *rationalisation* measures, provided the tools and principles through which *ahistorical* and *nonpolitical* 'technical difficulties' impeding growth could be presented as solvable (Cullather 2000: 645–6). More crucially, modernisation theories provided the explicit rationale upon which foreign aid government operates, that is: *aid* is needed to promote and achieve *development*.

DOI: 10.1057/9781137505903.0005

From the end of the 1950s up to the end of the 1960s there was solid support and confidence in the operations of the foreign aid system. Its own institutional spaces, organisations and structures had started to be established, and aid flows rose steadily. Aid was delivered in the form of short-term projects and technical and financial assistance that initially mainly focused on infrastructure and industry, but gradually started to concern health, education and agriculture as well (Eggen and Roland 2014: 22). Around the 1970s aid flows started to fall rapidly and foreign aid's many downsides started to be increasingly highlighted. From the 1960s the failure of modernisationists' prescriptions was increasingly acknowledged. It was increasingly pointed out by dependency and world system theories that the modernist approach was a reflection of the political and economic interests of Western powers (see Chapter 3). Revolutionary movements and institutions dominated by developing countries called for a more equitable and inclusive international order – a 'New International Economic Order'. In response to the 'cynical attitude' present in both developed and developing countries in relation 'not only to the effectiveness of the aid effort, but about the validity of the very concept of aid' (Pearson 1970: 6), the Pearson Report (1969)[5] was produced. It was the first institutional effort out of many produced over the years to improve and sustain the truth of development.[6] Its tone and main content, which would be more or less effectively replicated in the subsequent international reports on the matter, can be effectively summarised by also looking at Pearson's 1970 address to the World Bank. By calling attention to the crucial 'point of decision' reached by international aid efforts and to what it had already achieved in terms of growth and progress, Pearson highlighted that such an effort was not only 'practicable' but 'of essential importance' and therefore should not be put into question. The main question, Pearson confidently said, was not *whether* development would happen or not, but *when* and at what pace. Development for developing countries, he argued, was in fact no longer 'an option' but 'an imperative' – 'another stage in their struggle for freedom' – and in this sense they had 'no choice' but to move towards development. As for developed countries *that did have a choice*, aid was to be acknowledged, in the first place, as based on a 'humanitarian and moral concern' derived from 'the duty of the rich and the privileged to help the poor and the deprived', and therefore as the result of the 'natural obligations of community'. In the second place, it was to be recognised as a requirement of the 'increasingly close and *interdependent* world

DOI: 10.1057/9781137505903.0005

community'; a requirement that did not dismiss the importance of national self-interest as the basis of every policy but that implied that national self-interest must be 'enlightened and farsighted', and capable of looking beyond its boundaries (1970: 6–7, emphasis added). In this light, the Pearson Report called for a renewed recognition by donor countries of the truth that cooperation with other states and the assurance of 'basic social and economic conditions' to all men (1970: 8) was crucial to prevent war – that development was still the new name of peace. By taking stock of the limitations of foreign aid practices, of the intrinsic threats that development posed to developing countries' stability and unity and its 'disruptive' nature, Pearson also argued for a twofold change in the approach to development. This change was to be based, firstly, on a genuine '*partnership*' between rich nations and poor ones and on clear limitations of the former's intervention in the policy making of the latter (1969: 7, emphasis added). Secondly, it was to be based on adequate aid flows that *quantitatively* should reach the target of 0.7 per cent of GNP (that would soon become the official target to be reached) and that should be accompanied with equally important policies on trade and private capital flows. From a *qualitative* point of view, aid should no longer be based on the donors' 'narrow' political, military and commercial interests but it should focus on improving developing countries' *economic performance*. Aid should be better organised and administered based on a 'systematic approach'. It should be allocated according to 'explicit criteria', and towards 'tangible' objectives of economic growth without ignoring 'social change' (1970: 6–10).

The change in approach to development Pearson called for was brought about in the same decade, mainly by the World Bank and the International Labour Organisation, and was given the names of 'redistribution-with-growth' approach and 'basic needs' approach, respectively. By challenging the equation between economic growth and development, and the assumption that economic growth and structural innovation would indirectly lead, through the so called trickle–down effect, to a reduction of poverty, these argumentations (yet in different ways) inserted, for the first time, the fight against *poverty* and the attention to *growth redistribution* within the discourse and space of action of development. By suggesting that poverty should be at the centre of debate and action, they also put forward the idea that development processes and procedures should aim at directly targeting *poor people* (see Ghai et al. 1980, Binns 2008: 85, Riddell 2007: 88–9).

DOI: 10.1057/9781137505903.0005

A crucial shift in development truth, discourse and knowledge began in the beginning of the 1980s when the application of the neoliberal 'cure' to both developed and developing economies led to the implementation of Structural Adjustment Programmes (SAPs). In this period the World Bank redefined development no longer as economic growth but as successful 'participation in the world market' (World Bank quoted in Robinson 2002: 1056) thus opening the way to the complex set of changes that would be informed by free trade, growth and efficiency imperatives and would become known as the 'Washington consensus'. In the name of the need to comply with the requirements of economic interdependence, national economies of the Third World underwent a radical process of reform through 'stabilisation' and 'adjustment' measures designed by the International Monetary Fund (IMF) and the World Bank (WB), whose main objectives were: *macroeconomic stability, liberalisation* of trade and finances, *deregulation, fiscal discipline, privatisation* (Robinson 2002: 1057). 'Getting the prices right' was the core motivation of these measures (Eggen and Roland 2014: 27).

The sadly known effects of neoliberal cure, austerity programmes and the drastic elimination of state intervention and spending, gave rise to a tense period of confrontation, social and political protests and ideological contestation, which led to a deep credibility crisis of development strategy (Marshall et al. 2001, Robinson 2002, Eggen and Roland 2014). They also paved the way for a complex, technically sophisticated and discursively powerful process of strategic change that would lead to a radical shift in the governmental rationality of the foreign aid regime.

A first indication of this shift is provided by a brief analysis of the ways in which the 'technologies' of *conditionality, ownership, participation* and *good governance*, as Anders calls them (2005: 40), were designed and operationalised after the crisis induced by the SAPs. In the technical world of the *unaccountable* foreign aid regime, the need to make recipient countries *accountable*, to make sure they would do 'their job', has been a constant concern. This concern had taken the form, in the earliest phases of the development of the foreign aid system, of policy requirements linked to the cold-war logic, or of other policy and macroeconomic basic requirements as conditions to obtain aid (Eggen and Roland 2014: 24). This embryonic form of 'strings attached' evolved into the policy conditionality characteristic of the early 1980s, which was more elaborated as well as highly criticised. In this phase, conditionality included the realisation of 'hard' neoliberal policy reforms and infrastructure investments

DOI: 10.1057/9781137505903.0005

(Lie 2005: 5). In technical terms, the WB and the IMF developed four types of conditionality, namely *prior actions*, *performance criteria*, *quantitative performance criteria* and *structural benchmarks*. The first two criteria were intended as 'hard' conditions, in the sense that they had to be met by borrowing countries for the loan to be disbursed (Anders 2005: 51).

More than a decade later, the Poverty Reduction Strategy Papers (PRSPs) replaced the SAPs as new preconditions for obtaining loans and debt relief from the WB and the IMF. Contrary to the 'hard' reforms of the 1980s, those of the 1990s did not give rise to protest or debate. They involved all foreign aid actors, and particularly those NGOs and civil society organisations that had protested against economic liberalisation and hard conditionality (Eggen and Roland 2014: 50–1, Gould 2005: 62).

The PRSPs are now 'a condition of most grant aid and concessional lending' to the poorest countries of the world as also other donors (such as bilateral ones) are requested to coordinate their aid through them (Marshall et al. 2001: 1–2). The PRSPs are nominally focused on *reducing poverty* and are informed by the need to ensure the *participation* of recipient countries as well as the country *ownership* of development strategies and programmes. The intention is to reverse the 'traditional' top-down aid relationship. To move beyond the donor-imposed hard conditions of SAPs by putting recipient governments 'in the driver's seat' and by giving them the power to take charge of their development (Lie 2005: 1, 10). In order to be 'owned' by recipient countries, the PRSPs have to be prepared *by* recipient governments through a participatory process involving many stakeholders including actors from civil society and donors. These stakeholders should be involved at all levels of the process: from planning and management, to implementation, follow-up and reporting (2005: 4). Governments however remain the sole entity responsible and accountable for the PRSPs. Most crucially, the PRSPs *have to be approved by donors* (2005: 11–13).

In this way, as highlighted by Lie, through the operation of the inter-linked technologies of ownership and participation it is not power that is consigned to recipients, but rather 'responsibility and accountability' (2005: 13). Whereas recipient countries know very well that in order to get their PRSP document accepted, and thus to obtain aid, they have to propose to do what donors want them to do, in the new governmental architecture they are requested to do so 'voluntarily' (2005: 3). The unsolvable tension between the notions and intrinsic logic of ownership, on the one hand, and conditionality, on the other, is solved in the foreign

DOI: 10.1057/9781137505903.0005

aid regime by *unifying* them. Recipient governments are therefore made to put in *writing* the conditions to which they *voluntarily* commit themselves (see Anders 2005). Constituted as the sole responsible actors of the process, recipients become 'accomplices' in donor-driven policies and intentions (see Gould 2005). They become *actors* of, instead of subjects to, these policies and intentions.

As well articulated by Anders, the redesigned technology of conditionality/ownership is thus used 'to implant' good governance in recipient countries (2005: 40). The PRSPs in fact replace previous 'hard' conditionality with seemingly 'soft' conditionality, namely with *good governance* measures.[7] Good governance emerged as a central concept in development discourse in the 1990s, and it still represents the 'password' without which it 'has become virtually impossible to qualify for international foreign aid' (2005: 37). Just like participation and country ownership, it has been constructed by donors as an aid *effectiveness* and *performance* parameter, as a new remedy for aid inefficiency and dependency, and therefore a remedy for poverty and underdevelopment (2005: 37). In this sense, good governance is 'concerned with transforming "dysfunctional" state bureaucracies into efficient and transparent service-providers that are accountable to the public and subject to the rule of law' (2005: 37). It consists in a 'cluster of policy ideas' (Archer quoted in Lie 2005: 6) that, along with transparency and accountability, mainly mean 'checks on corruption and human rights abuses', 'political decentralisation' and 'multiparty democracy' (Pomerantz quoted in Lie 2005: 6).

Whereas good governance thus represents the new, technical and 'soft' *content* of conditionality, conditionality/ownership creates the 'legitimate', *technical* conditions for the good governance agenda to be operationalised. It is through the conditions they have themselves *written* that recipient governments commit themselves to adhere to the good governance agenda. In this way, the fact that good governance tools and models are designed by donors is not seen as a contradiction with recipient governments' ownership, autonomy and sovereignty because it is presented as a needed form of *technical* assistance from specialised agencies (Anders 2005: 47). Through this sophisticated structure of interlocking technologies, the governmental rationality of foreign aid regime has thus moved from the *direct*, 'external controls of conditionality' under SAPs to the *indirect*, 'internal discipline of PRSPs' (Mosse 2005a: 8, emphasis added). Powers of surveillance, monitoring and control over recipient states have become more efficient and intrusive through the

DOI: 10.1057/9781137505903.0005

responsibilisation of recipients. As highlighted by Lie, recipient governments are 'responsibilised' in order to be able to 'to develop, govern and control themselves' (2005: 16).

The above described technologies can be considered, drawing from Dean, as forms of 'technologies of performance'. These are technologies that aim to make the capacities of various actors 'calculable and comparable so that they might be optimized' (2010: 202). Through different technical means – from assessment, performance and benchmarking tools, to monitoring, accounting and reporting procedures and schemes – recipients of aid are in fact *indirectly* regulated. They are transformed into ' "calculating" ' actors 'within "calculable spaces"', subject to multiple and sophisticated ' "calculative regimes" ' (Dean 2010: 197 quoting Miller). These 'calculative regimes' are designed by donors to measure recipients' performance in different fields (from good governance, human rights, corruption to participation and accountability), and by using various indicators.

These technologies are typically interlinked with various 'technologies of agency' which Dean defines as technologies aimed at enhancing 'the capacities for participation, agreement and action' (Dean 2010: 202).[8] In the foreign aid regime, a crucial technology of agency is constituted by *capacity-building* techniques. As illustrated by Gould, this technology is constructed with the aim of making the achievement of good governance, ownership/conditionality and participation *possible*. Justified by the need to improve the *performance* of recipient actors at multiple levels and in varied sectors, capacity-building can provide entry 'into virtually any domain or arena: any subject, irrespective of other qualities, can be described with reference to its (lack of) capacity'. These can be ministries, legislative institutions and administrative structures. They can also range from private organisations, NGOs and advocacy networks, to groups of population (women, children, AIDS victims, indigenous people, farmers, and so on) (Gould 2005: 71, 70). By building upon 'the infinite improvability of the subject' – for 'there is no end to the extent to which one can acquire new capacities' – capacity-building gives rise to a multiplicity of practices that are linked to the specific objectives of the aid industry, and that imply 'a hierarchy of authority and expertise' (2005: 71). In this sense, capacity-building techniques complement the operation of the technologies of performance by 'instilling internalised disciplines of *good self-governance*' (2005: 70, emphasis added), in other words the capacity to self-monitor and self-regulate various aspects of

DOI: 10.1057/9781137505903.0005

the individual and collective conduct in order to *comply* with donors' demands and expectations.

The PRSPs are an example of the crucial role and influence exerted by the WB and the IMF in problematising and reshaping the governmental strategy of the foreign aid regime. Many of the imperatives included in the PRSPs – from human rights, democracy and good governance to ownership and participation – however also represent the areas where the operations of these financial institutions *strategically intersected* with the approach and goals of other foreign aid actors. Particularly since the end of the Cold War and thus with the 'end of political aid', high on the agenda of many actors within the foreign aid system were human rights imperatives and democracy principles. Some examples of initiatives and actors upholding these principles are: the so-called Stockholm Initiative which was promoted by four different international commissions;[9] the UNDP (United Nations Development Programme); the many non-governmental organisations (NGOs) which had started to play a progressively relevant role within the aid industry since the 1980s; social movements in many developing countries, and some donor countries or organisations, such as Scandinavian countries and the European Union. In the context of this '*moral* resurrection of aid' (Mosse 2005a: 1, emphasis added), development was renamed as 'sustainable' and 'human' and it was thus required to complement the attention to the quantity of growth with the attention to its *quality*, namely, environmental sustainability concerns, respect for human rights and democracy principles, human capabilities imperatives and human security objectives.[10]

Since the 1990s, donors from states, to multilateral organisations and NGOs increasingly engaged in supporting democratisation processes that had started in many developing countries after the end of the Cold War, and shifted attention to the need to reform the bureaucratic administration, institutions and society of recipient countries. Instead of aiming at 'getting the price right', they started to aim at 'getting state, policies, institutions, society, and people right' (Eggen and Roland 2014: 29). In the context of this renewed governmental strategy, instead of continuing to assume the form of projects, foreign aid rapidly started to assume the form of broad, sector-wide programs and direct budget support. Over just a few decades, the *reform* of recipient states, including their institutions, policies and society, has thus been constructed as the key and the preliminary step to move towards development, to obtain growth, the reduction of poverty and all the other proclaimed objectives

DOI: 10.1057/9781137505903.0005

of development. Foreign aid practices have rapidly become a tool to address recipient countries' and populations' many 'capacity' gaps; a 'tool for transformation of recipients'; a tool to realise political, institutional and social engineering (Eggen and Roland 2014: 29, 45). Over these few decades, the state shifted from being seen as the *solution*, to being seen as the *problem* and then to being seen as a crucial, strategic *part of the solution* (Brinkerhoff 2008: 986–7).

By looking at the ways in which foreign aid knowledge has changed over the years three stages have been identified. The first period of foreign aid interventions ranges from the end of the Second World War to the mid-1970s. It was the period of large infrastructure projects and state led development, thus the 'era of the *engineers*'. The second period spans from the mid-1970s to the late 1980s and was the period of the Washington consensus, of the belief in the power of open market and in the weakness of the state affirmed by neoclassicists – thus the era of '*economists*'. The third is the current period which was opened by PRSPs and people centred development and can thus be termed as the era of '*social scientists*' (Soesastro 2004: 6).

In the current era of 'social scientists' a particular body of theory has provided the epistemological grounds and the substance for the new role for foreign aid – the 'new institutional economics', which political scientists term as the 'new political economy' (Robinson 2002: 1058). Whereas the economic 'content' of development is still mainly informed by the priorities of the Washington consensus, this complementary theory has been deployed to better *manage* social and legal rules that underlie economic choices, and its influence is clearly reflected by the current emphasis on 'good governance'. Based on an assumption put forward by rational choice theory that social behaviour may be explained by 'the interplay of individuals pursuing their own best interests and "preferences" on the basis of rational choices and available information', this approach has enriched the dominant neoliberal, macroeconomic paradigm by focusing on the need to analyse how institutional arrangements may hinder or enhance the *economic* behaviour of agents and therefore development processes (Robinson 2002: 1058). Resonating well with modernisation theories, it assumes that obstacles to development are located not in the international structure but in the *agency* to be modified at the *institutional* level. In this perspective, development processes (social behaviour) may be *modelled* and their constraints may be modified and removed by *efficient* institutions, namely institutions able to

DOI: 10.1057/9781137505903.0005

provide individuals with adequate *incentives* to improve their economic behaviour (2002: 1059). The main assumption is that '*institutional change can be considered at the heart of the long-run process of economic development, providing the missing link between development* and *growth*' (Mustapha and Nugent quoted in Robison 2002: 1059, emphasis added). As promoting institutional reform is a 'risky business', it is not about 'bricks and mortar' but about 'reshaping *values, principles* and *interests*, and redefining underlying *power relations*' (Rocha Menocal 2013: 2, emphasis added), proper *technical* tools, methodologies and schemes are thus required, designed and searched. In this broad and rich field, a particularly indicative example is offered by *political economy analysis*. In a recent UNDP Guidance note on Institutional and Context Analysis (ICA), which is grounded on assumptions similar to those that underpin political economy analyses, it is for instance stated:

> Among the most important lessons we have learned since the 1990s is that progress towards human development requires *a change in power relations*. A *new social contract* that underpins state–society relations and widens the democratic space can catalyse transformation.
>
> Changing power relations requires a *clear understanding of who is powerful, why, who is not, and why*. It requires *careful reading of the institutional and political factors that promote or block development and include or exclude societies' poor and marginalized people*. Too often, development has tended to focus on technical assistance alone rather than *on the enabling or disabling environment in a country or sector or across sectors*. As a result, many technically sound development programmes failed to achieve their intended results.
>
> This Guidance Note was developed to strengthen support for practitioners on the *political economy of change*. [...] As demonstrated by recent transitions in the Arab world, this understanding is critical for us to engage effectively with the *positive agents of change* in the countries where we work. [...]
>
> [*ICA*] [...] focuses attention on *incentives, relationships* and the *distribution* and contest of power between *groups* and *individual women and men, because all have a significant impact on development outcomes*. The process should include *the use of data and information that are disaggregated by sex, age and other important variables*. (2012: vi, 10, emphasis added)

The assumption of an ICA is that 'development requires a change in power relations and/or incentive systems'; it requires therefore nothing less than a 'new social contract'. In this context, the *technical* focus is on mapping, scrutinising and understanding individual and collective actors' *interests, incentives* and *constraints*. This will demonstrate how they may challenge

DOI: 10.1057/9781137505903.0005

development programmes, 'where the obstacles are and how to address them'. Attention is therefore given to the identification of different types and sources of *risk* and on their *management* and *assessment* in order to identify the 'positive agents of change' (UNDP 2012: 1, 7, vi).

Another component of the new rationality of government of the foreign aid regime has been effectively identified and scrutinised by Duffield (2001a) under the caption 'privatisation'. This is seen firstly in how the rationality of the foreign aid regime has been 'marketised' (2001a: 308): by reinforcing public–private networks and partnership at (g)local levels, by increasingly looking for private sources of funding and by continuing to draw from the analysis and new management tools, technologies and strategies of the private sector (Kindornay and Reilly-King 2013).[11] Secondly, as Duffield points out, the shift towards the 'privatisation' of aid has been particularly sustained by the 'securitisation' of development and by the way in which security has been reconceptualised by Northern countries (2001a, see also Larzillière 2012).

Development and security were considered interstate affairs during the 1950s and the 1960s, and South countries were considered as strategic allies in the cold-war scenario. Since the end of the 1970s however recipient countries started to be increasingly seen for their inability to maintain security within their borders (2001a: 311). The security problems that affected them, from the varied forms of new, internal (ethnicity/identity based), regionalised and criminalised conflicts, to the refugee crises, were presented as deriving from their insufficient development. Developing countries thus started to be seen as potentially dangerous, as posing a constant, menacing threat (2001a: 311). On the one hand, this has led to the introduction of many security-related activities within development programmes. On the other hand, and more crucially, within the reshaped development–security nexus it is no longer (recipient) states' sovereignty per se that is seen as 'the locus of security', but rather, in line with the redesigned strategy of the foreign aid regime, 'the nature and quality of [their] *domestic relations*' (Duffield 2001a: 311, see Duffield 2001b, 2007). In this context, as further highlighted by Duffield, whereas recipient states are constructed as 'things to be "reformed" or "reconstructed"', the whole Third World becomes visible as a potentially dangerous 'social body' to be controlled, carefully monitored and regulated (Duffield 2001a: 311). The theoretical framework that creates the conditions for the insertion of security concerns *within* the renewed strategy of foreign aid practices that we have analysed earlier is provided by the concept of 'human security'. As Duffield effectively explains:

> The *social diagnostics* associated with ideas of human security constitute the points of intervention where metropolitan actors attempt to modulate the behaviour of the populations involved. [...] The securitisation of development denotes a situation in which the *security* concerns of metropolitan states have merged with the *social* concerns of aid agencies; they have become one and the same thing. (Duffield 2001a: 311–12, emphasis added)

Privatisation has thus become the new, additional governmental strategy through which the foreign aid regime operates to address both its *social* and its closely interlinked, almost indistinguishable, reshaped *security* concerns. In this light, the higher ambitions and goals require the engagement of a wide range of 'specialist non-state and private organisations' and therefore the operationalisation of multiple, open and extremely varied public–private networks (Duffield 2001a: 312). This renewed strategy mainly involves the engagement of NGOs, different transnational civil society networks, associations, private multinational companies and agencies, and private security companies. Through the techniques of 'partnership frameworks' and 'global compacts',[12] of 'contracting-out' activities and projects and of 'subcontracting arrangements' (Duffield 2001a: 310), various Northern and Southern non-state actors have been 'governmentalized' as a constitutive, yet 'self-managing', component of the foreign aid regime (Duffield 2007: 25, see Silk 2004: 238). These actors are engaged in raising the level of *compliance* of recipient societies and individuals with the liberal model of civil society and active citizens, but they are also engaged in reducing societies and individuals' level of *vulnerability* (Duffield 2001a: 312–14, see Eggen and Roland 2014: 50–1). The securitisation of development has in fact also meant the operationalisation of the 'rationality of risk' and its many tools, analysis methodologies and management techniques (see Dean 2010: 205–27). Rather than being in contradiction with the technologies previously analysed, the rationality of risk has become increasingly bound up with the technologies of agency and performances. The ways in which they are assembled and simultaneously operationalised is vividly described in the latest World Bank's World Development Report 2014 (WDR 2014) aptly entitled *Risk and Opportunity – Managing Risk for Development*:

> *The WDR 2014 argues that risk management can be a powerful instrument for development – not only by building people's resilience and thus reducing*

DOI: 10.1057/9781137505903.0005

the effects of adverse events but also by allowing them to take advantage of opportunities for improvement. [...]

The solution is not to reject change in order to avoid risk but to prepare for the opportunities and risks that change entails. Managing risks responsibly and effectively has the potential to bring about security and a means of progress for people in developing countries and beyond. (WDR 2014: 3)

In this renewed context, *calculating* and managing risks represent a crucial component of 'development management'. Risk is conceived as both a 'burden' and an 'opportunity', and risk management is intended as a *'proactive, systematic, and integrated approach'* that should *actively* involve households, communities, enterprises, financial system and states in recipient countries, as well as the international community (2014: 4, 3). The focus is on the *knowledge, (self-)protection* and *(self-)insurance* measures/policies, and *coping* strategies that can allow these various actors to 'combine the capacity to prepare for risk with the ability to cope afterward' (2014: 12). Particular attention is given to the techniques, measures and mechanisms that can improve and 'optimise' the level of *resilience*, probably one of the most recent technologies of agency in the foreign aid field, of both different social and economic collective actors and groups of individuals (see Duffield 2013). At the level of strategy, techniques of risk assessment and management allow for a shift from a deontological, duty-based logic to a consequentialist one 'that subordinates actions to the calculus of possible outcomes' (Duffield 2001a: 315, see also Larzillière 2012: 9). In this sense, they have also contributed to give rise to particular forms of *spatialisation*.

The marketisation of aid makes it possible to divide recipient territories into *non-profitable* and *profitable* sites for foreign investment. Risk analysis and mapping tools on the other hand allow the separation of the world into *'pre-modern* "zones of chaos" ' and *'modern* and *post-modern* zones of order' (Dean 2010: 246 quoting Cooper, emphasis added). In addition, risk analysis tools allow to further disaggregate the 'zones of chaos' into 'various factors of threat and vulnerability' (Duffield 2001a: 314). Fragmentation, stratification and *selective* inclusion are amongst the terms used to describe the complex effects of these different but closely interlinked forms of social/economic and geographical spatialisation (Ludden 2005: 16–17, Mosse 2005a: 12). As a result, Third World countries, particularly *failed*, 'weak' ones, have thus been increasingly produced as composed of multiple, ever-expanding and constantly changing (zones of) potential threats that put interdependence in an

DOI: 10.1057/9781137505903.0005

irremediable situation of constant insecurity and uncertainty. This situation has justified a *legitimate* level of intrusion control, optimisation and regulation *within* recipient countries, which is 'unprecedented since the colonial period' (Duffield 2001a: 311). As noted by Duffield, in this sense the foreign aid regime has undergone a 'biopolitical turn'. In the name of both productivity and security imperatives, it has become a contemporary example of *biopolitics* that divides populations into both territorial and non-territorial groups according to the 'capacities, deficiencies and potentialities' of the people. It provides incentives, it selects, modulates and supports 'positive' capacities, choices and potentialities, and it discourages the 'negative' ones in order to 'optimise' the population of governed countries (Tschirhart 2011: 6, see Duffield 2007).

After the launch of the global war on terror, foreign aid practices have become the tool to enhance 'global security' and 'global governance'. To ensure the *conservation* of order against global *fears* while pointing to the (renewed) possibility of *transforming* the global order in the name of new, global *hopes* – such as for instance those connected to the adoption of the 'global public goods' approach and to the achievement of the Millenium Development Goals (see Kaul et al. 1999, Riddell 2007, Severino and Ray 2009). The importance of development *truth*, *discourse* and *knowledge* in relation to foreign aid governmental various rationalities, techniques and strategies could hardly be overemphasised. Thinking, talking and attempting to practically reach development means in fact to talk, think and attempt to practice a *change*. More precisely, it is to think, talk and attempt to translate into practice the 'intent' to change and to move towards better conditions. As Cowen and Shenton crucially point out: 'the existence of an intent to develop does mean that it is believed that it is possible to act in the name of development and that it is believed that development will follow from actions deemed desirable to realise an intention of development' (1996: viii). When problems, limitations, negative outcomes and dramatic consequences arise, it is not the 'intent' to develop that is questioned, but it is something around it, beyond or below it – be it the inadequateness of its goals, theoretical framework or related strategies. Under the intention to develop, it is not foreign aid interventions *per se* that are questioned but rather their *technical* limitations. Under the intention to develop there is always room for new issues to be protected, *conserved*, and new aspects to be changed, *transformed*.

DOI: 10.1057/9781137505903.0005

Countries and peoples that cannot be trusted

> *Imperare sibi maximum imperium est.*
>
> (Seneca, *Moral Letters to Lucilius, 113: 31*)

The foreign aid system operates through the actions of different actors, each of which is constructed with its own role and specific authority, 'identity', reputation and available tools. Since the 1960s and the 1970s many developed countries and newly independent ones entered the foreign aid scene that until then had been dominated by the United States and colonial powers. Donor countries started to establish domestic specialised agencies and institutions to coordinate and implement development policies, frequently by 'refreshing' their colonial administration agencies and personnel (see Kothari 2005, Unger 2010, Frey and Kunkel 2011). New international programmes were established (for instance, the World Food Programme or the UNDP) to join forces with the many other institutions, specialised agencies and organisations that had already started to increasingly engage in the development endeavour (the WB, the IMF, the Food and Agriculture Organisation (FAO), the International Labour Organisation (ILO), the Organisation for Economic Co-operation and Development (OECD)).[13] Currently the United Nations alone count close to 70 organisations or funds dedicated to development that just like development ideas and theories, emerge and with difficulty disappear (Severino and Ray 2009: 6). The European Union has increasingly become an important donor, donor countries' specialised agencies have flourished and many other countries (Eastern countries like Russia, Bulgaria, Romania and Latvia, and Asian countries like China, Malaysia) have joined the scene as donors after having been recipients for years (Riddell 2007, Stokke 2009, Severino and Ray 2009). Since around the 1980s NGOs have become important and recognised actors in the official aid system. Over the years they consistently emerged, also in recipient countries, as actors on the micro level through direct involvement in development projects as well as at transnational level (Skøtt Thomsen 2007: 23–6). More recently, an expanding number of varied non-state, private actors have become part of the system.

Such a complex context has always been particularly fragmented and peculiarly competitive. On the one hand, foreign aid has always been a field of rivalry in which Western governments confronted many competitors: the Soviet Union until the end of the Cold War; Southern

DOI: 10.1057/9781137505903.0005

countries during the 1970s as a result of the developing countries' efforts to collectively take the scene and to orient foreign aid towards the creation of a New International Economic Order; in more recent years, the 'Washington model' of aid has been increasingly challenged by the so-called Beijing model (see Eggen and Roland 2014: 94–102). But *competition*, along with *negotiation*, is also an essential source of vitality *within* the foreign aid regime. Every donor country has its own priorities and defends its spheres of influence and action – it competes, it negotiates with other donors in local spaces of interventions in order to establish relations of *'alliance'* and *'precedence'* that reverberate on the global domain (Silva 2008: 2, emphasis added*)*. The same happens in relation to development agencies and bodies at national and international levels that have, just like any other bureaucratic organisation, their own peculiar profile and mission. Together with negotiating spaces of alliance with the other actors, they bring forward their own strategies and attempts to defend their specialised mandates, roles, functions, and their leadership and position.

In relation to this, it has been highlighted that *credibility* is a crucial asset in the dynamics of power allocation within the foreign aid regime. Indeed, it is the source of both *recognition* and *funding* (Gould 2005: 77, 79).

In the context of the foreign aid industry, multilateral organisations are overall deemed to offer a more 'neutral channel' for aid resources. This is due to their 'multilateral' nature and, particularly in the case of agencies and programmes of the United Nations, because they anchor their actions to the values and principles enshrined in the UN Charter (Black 2004: 46–7, Stokke 2009). Soon after their involvement in the foreign aid endeavour, the United Nations started to exercise a critical influence through their agenda setting role by assuming the authority, together with the OECD and other multilateral organisations, intergovernmental bodies and the development 'epistemic community', to define the objectives, principles and directions towards which foreign aid practices should move. In this way, they have all contributed to ensuring that development truth and knowledge continue to evolve and to be constantly realigned to the new emerging 'trends' and 'interests' (Nederveen Pieterse 2002, Stokke 2009, Maul 2009). The PRSPs that we have analysed earlier represent the way in which the WB and the IMF have attempted to reconstitute their image and enhance their *credibility* as poverty-oriented institutions after the crises induced by the SAPs (Gould 2005: 74). They also represent an example of how all

DOI: 10.1057/9781137505903.0005

development agencies and institutions work hard to preserve their credibility. In the case of UN agencies, they are financially dependent on *voluntary* contributions, first and foremost from member governments. This makes them, on the one hand, subject to strong political pressure.[14] On the other hand, they have to *persuade* donor countries to contribute. In order to gain donor countries' *trust* they are therefore very careful not to taint their 'good image' (see Stokke 2009: 482).

The same dynamic applies to NGOs. On the one hand, NGOs' avowed role and media profile is that of 'ethics and values organizations' that *really* care (Silk 2004: 238), especially because they are commonly held to play a critical ' "gap-filling" role' within the foreign aid system (Skøtt Thomsen 2007: 22). According to this perspective, they fill many operational, efficiency and accountability gaps by injecting pluralism and democratisation imperatives into the practice and theory of aid. They also promote 'real' partnership and active participation of 'beneficiaries' through the adoption of a human rights-based approach. They are more close and more consistently oriented towards the needs and social problems of people. And finally they provide basic social services at grassroots level in a more efficient and flexible manner (2007: 21–8).

On the other hand, the NGOs' world is a fragmented and pluralistic one, in which funding is crucial towards NGOs' own financial sustainability, and competition for funds is constantly on the increase. Their level of financial dependency, which may vary depending on their dimensions and geographic reach, together with their 'contract culture' and consistent levels of socialisation and assimilation into the donors' technology and culture (see previous section), have increasingly produced an identity and credibility crisis for NGOs due to contradictions between their image and practical role (Silk 2004: 238, see Ferguson and Gupta 2002: 993–4). As a result, NGOs have attempted to reinforce their position by increasingly engaging in developing transnational *networks* and initiatives and in strengthening their ties with the market sector and with varied actors in the South ranging from grassroots organisations to social movements (Silk 2004: 241, see Skøtt Thomsen 2007: 28–31). They have relied on their 'direct links to the grassroots' and their connections with national and transnational networks to reaffirm and consolidate their credibility (Gould 2005: 77).

In the foreign aid regime, *credibility* remains however a prerogative and a resource that is mainly, albeit variably, assigned to donors. This becomes particularly evident when looking at the ways in which

DOI: 10.1057/9781137505903.0005

accountability dynamics operate within the system. It is widely acknowledged that in spite of the huge emphasis on accountability and transparency the foreign aid regime builds upon a fundamental accountability gap or deficit. In contrast to domestic interventions where citizens or residents in a state can hold their governments accountable, foreign aid interventions are directed towards beneficiaries who do not hold a formal entitlement to hold donor governments accountable for their actions. And this is not mentioning multilateral organisations and other non-state actors. In the domestic setting, 'at home', taxpayers have a right to hold a state accountable but they do not have direct experience and knowledge of what is being done miles away from them. They therefore have to rely on the evaluation, assessment and measurement-of-giving efforts elaborated by donors themselves or at best by fully fledged development experts (Eyben 2005: 100).

On the contrary, the foreign aid regime operates upon the upward (meaning towards the donors) accountability of its various actors, networks and partners. More crucially, it operates through the upward accountability of recipient governments, that through foreign aid practices are constructed as the actors to be blamed for the persistent failures, problems and negative consequences of aid interventions. Being, according to Bauer's definition, 'a transfer of resources from the *taxpayer* of a donor country to the *government* of a recipient country' (Bauer quoted in Shleifer 2009: 379–80), foreign aid hinders and/or alters the domestic accountability of recipient countries' governments, and for many years it has sustained aligned dictators, oppressive, authoritarian political leaders and regimes, clientelism and the private appropriation by political elites of 'development' resources (Hancock 1989, Moss et al. 2006). By breaking the link between government resources and tax revenue, foreign aid undermines the establishment or preservation of the basic contract between government and governed as it is based on the 'no taxation without representation' principle (Knack 2004, Black 2004, Moss et al. 2006, Shleifer 2009). By being on both ends of the aid relationship burdened with serious corruption and misappropriation phenomena, foreign aid poses a further challenge to the possibility of ensuring transparency and accountability on both the donors' and the recipients' sides (Hancock 1989, Black 2004, Moyo 2009). Many ethnographies have shown how foreign aid works at the local level through complex, flexible, multidimensional processes of negotiations, interactions and shifting alliances, where personality, social networks and

DOI: 10.1057/9781137505903.0005

relationships are the most important factors for both donor and recipient actors (see Mosse 2005a). The proliferation and fragmentation of donors' missions, the very consistent number of aid agencies and NGOs that operate simultaneously within recipient countries,[15] nurtures multiple and ever shifting spaces of interaction where the level of 'harmonisation' of aid interventions, and therefore donor and recipient actors' room to manoeuvre, may vary (see Eyben 2005: 102).

Thus whereas foreign aid produces processes that 'disperse accountability and maximise deniability' (Mosse 2005a: 16 quoting Wedel), its governmental strategy functions by constructing upward accountability as a *measurable* domain, at all levels and through complex technologies (see previous section). More crucially, although these technologies are designed to reinforce *credibility* and not the accountability of donor actors, they also *construct* and sustain the *unaccountability* (and lack of credibility) of recipient states. Recipient states (and populations) that therefore become overall intrinsically *untrustworthy*.

In relation to the question of *trust*, the literature on gift provides some precious insights into the peculiar way in which foreign aid relationships, as gift relationships, construct their main actors. Whereas a certain degree of trust is required to establish any type of formal or informal relationship, Verhezen has highlighted that trust in itself works in a paradoxical way for it is in fact highly necessary when a relationship is to be developed in the absence of formal rules and conventions, of conditions of certainty and of clear information. The more the formal rules, guarantees and information that are made available, the more sensibly predictable is the outcome of a relationship, and therefore the lesser degree of trust that is needed to initiate and construct such a relationship (2005: 162–3). The notion of trust is thus vital to a gift relationship: not only is the initial gift an expression of trust in the possibility to develop cooperation and reciprocity, but it is also an attempt to produce a peculiar form of trust-based relationship in which the uncertainty is not only assumed as a constitutive element, but is also continuously maintained and stimulated through debt and non-equivalence in order 'to allow trust to blossom' (2005: 38) and therefore in order to nourish the *transformative* potential of gift. On the contrary, the foreign aid relationship is based on the donors' *conservative* attempt to minimise the level of uncertainty, to charge recipients with the burden of uncertainty and to make the eventual 'blossoming' of trust closely dependent on the recipients' level of *compliance* with the conditions attached to the

DOI: 10.1057/9781137505903.0005

foreign aid gift. In this sense, it has been effectively highlighted that donors intend the aid relationship as a *contractual* relationship.[16] A particularly convenient contractual relationship in which recipients can be sanctioned through exclusion or a reduction of aid flows if they do not comply with the conditionality requirements and, on the contrary, donors cannot be sanctioned if they do not respect their commitments in terms of *quantity* and/or *quality* of aid (Eyben 2005: 100, see Anders 2005). Even though the aid relationship includes contractual elements such as loans (but see Anders 2005), the fact that it is not based on equivalence and symmetry and is not governed by the law makes the aid relationship not a contractual relationship but a proper gift relationship, albeit a peculiar one.

Although with an element of trust, *mutual* accountability and real partnership (another crucial keyword in the foreign aid regime) are extremely likely to arise (Watt 2005, Eyben 2005), within a 'conditional-trust' scheme the burden of trust (and accountability) is entirely upon recipients. It is up to them to demonstrate that they are trustable. Which they may become only if they are *compliant,* that is, if they self-govern, self-control and self-regulate themselves according to donors' prescriptions. In short, recipient governments' trustworthiness is constructed as something that does not exist. As something that can be endlessly *improved* through development tools and policies, namely through capacity-building actions. In contrast, donors' trustworthiness (and accountability) is a pre-assumption as they hold the power to define accountability standards and informational base, acceptable behaviour, performance indicators and any other criteria that measure *trust.* This is even more generously ascribed when they are some multilateral organisations or non-governmental actors. On the other hand, recipient countries are under the effect of an invasive, managerial and 'tyrannous' set of technologies that aim at making their (un)trustworthiness *visible* while leaving the ways in which trust/accountability is constructed *concealed* (Strathern 2000). In other words, concealing the ways in which foreign aid processes and technologies are the conditions that make possible the *practical* exercise of development as a form of moral, cultural, educative 'trusteeship' over recipient *countries, societies* and *populations* (see Cowen and Shenton 1996).

As highlighted by Gould (2005), along with applying to states, the dynamic of trust contributes to the activation of mechanisms of self-government and self-discipline also at the local level of practice. The need

DOI: 10.1057/9781137505903.0005

for donors to allocate a form of (continuously scrutinised and extremely volatile) trust to locally sustain the implementation of development policies leads to the establishment of local, *personal* alliances with selected 'individuals at the fulcra of power' who become temporary 'trustees' of the governing processes, and also a 'model of self-discipline for others' (Gould 2005: 68).

In relation to this and drawing from Foucault, Kapoor has applied the concept of 'panopticism' in order to illustrate the ways in which foreign aid practices reconstruct, by activating self-policing processes, the ways in which people interact, knowledge is exchanged, needs are constructed and expressed. Kapoor shows how through complex, relational processes, and at various levels, recipient government officials, elites, families, and particularly individuals and groups in a dominant position, may develop an 'interest' in aligning with the new regime truths to achieve consent, manage dissent or for other reasons. They may end up self-disciplining, that is, internalising such truths to a point when they become 'naturalized' and 'taken for granted' (2008: 68–9). Similarly, it has been highlighted by Eyben that the donor-centred audit culture produces a specific process of 'colonisation' over recipient countries' organisations that not only reshape their procedures and structures in order to provide the information required, but also adopt donors' parameters to describe themselves (Pentland, Power quoted in Eyben 2005: 102). 'Colonisation', Eyben highlights, may coexist with 'decoupling', that is an attitude of pretended formal compliance that is however not coupled with a real internalisation and appropriation of the new procedures, and which may lead to assume a secretive, deceptive attitude (Pentland quoted in Eyben 2005: 102). Colonisation may produce 'transformative' learning, that is, the assumption of a new point of view, or 'regressive' learning, that is, one of compliance (Vince quoted in Eyben 2005: 102).

Within the fragmented field opened by foreign aid practices, governmental strategies and technologies may exert varying levels of influence, (g)local alliances may shift, and each actor's room for manoeuvre may extend or diminish. Capacity-building may produce *real* empowerment, namely forms of creative or subversive application of the capacities apprehended (Gould 2005: 71).[17] Colonisation may produce 'resistance learning', a form of resistance that constitutes, as Eyben points out, 'the weapons of the weak' (2005: 102). The weapons of the weak against the technologically sophisticated weapons of the strong.

DOI: 10.1057/9781137505903.0005

The logic of the gift

Mundus vult decipi, ergo decipiatur.

Over the years, foreign aid practices have consistently and flexibly enlarged their scope. They have continuously enriched their methodologies and tools, absorbed new languages, included new spheres of actions and extended their explicit ambitions. Evolving from the first project-based phase, they have become mainly engaged in achieving broad, 'intangible' aims such as capacity-building, good governance, political, social and institutional reform of countries, human and global security. And whereas it is possible to verify the attainment of tangible, project-based results (infrastructures, services), the degree of success or failure in reaching such broader, 'intangible' aims cannot be 'quantitatively' assessed (Eggen and Roland 2014: 73–4).

Despite this, the foreign aid 'industry' has retained and expanded its solid obsession with numbers, indicators, measurement tools, performance, *effectiveness* and accountability metrics. It has developed sophisticated and specialist monitoring mechanisms and technical knowledge, and it has established, constantly improved and extended a specific 'culture of targets, benchmarking and aid effectiveness' (Macrae et al. 2004: 11–12, Roodman 2007, Eggen and Roland 2014). Whereas as we have already seen this 'obsession' represents a crucial component of the governmental rationality of the foreign aid regime, it also provides a useful entry point to the analysis of the intrinsic logic of the foreign aid regime. In this context, particularly relevant is the analysis of the ways in which the official measure according to which foreign aid practices are benchmarked and assessed, that is the Official Development Assistance (ODA), has been constructed and applied.

According to the official definition, for an expenditure to qualify, be eligible, and thus reportable as ODA, it must: originate from an official agency (states, local governments); be directed towards countries and territories on the Development Assistance Committee (DAC) List of ODA Recipients or to multilateral development institutions;[18] have a concessional character (with a grant element of at least 25%); and its 'main objective' must be the 'promotion of the economic development and welfare of developing countries'.[19] It is good to note that whereas the Development Assistance Committee (DAC) of the OECD was established

DOI: 10.1057/9781137505903.0005

by Euro-American powers at the very beginning of the institutionalisation of foreign aid practices, the main content of the current definition of the ODA was agreed upon after lengthy debates and negotiation rounds amongst DAC members only in 1972.

At the beginning of the aid enterprise, resource flows from donors to recipients included grants, loans, export credits, mixed credits, associated finance, private investments and other sources of finance without distinction. The need to distinguish concessional aid from other flows emerged in relation to the fact that official concessional aid was the only part of resource flows that was under governments' direct control (Hynes and Scott 2013: 3–4). The definition of the criteria that allow to qualify a resource flow as ODA – concessional terms, grant threshold and developmental intention – were (and still are) subject to tense debate and controversy, to varied practices from donors as well as to many proposals for reform. In relation to the 'developmental intention', for instance, the DAC Secretariat has over the years received many requests from members for rulings on the ODA eligibility of disparate expenditures such as pensions for former colonial officers, aid to resistance movements, and compensation for the expropriation (nationalisation) of assets (2013: 8).

Despite controversy and debate, the ODA remains the only legitimate standard to assess and measure foreign aid flows, a standard that is however extremely limited. On the one hand, as Severino and Ray highlight, it 'measures too much' (2009: 17), as it includes expenditures that do not reflect a substantial financial effort and do not relate directly to any development intention or real transfer of resources (for instance, donors' administrative costs, grants for university students from developing countries, cost of reception of refugees in donor countries, debt relief, cost of public information programmes to promote aid). On the other hand, it measures 'too little' and the 'wrong things', in that it does not allow to adequately reflect the profoundly changed landscape in which foreign aid has operated since the end of the Cold War (2009: 18–20). In this sense, according to many experts and scholars, a broader and more inclusive definition would be needed in terms of: objectives (by including all global public goods and global security-related measures); actors (by including relevant non-DAC donors, such as China[20]); additional resources flows (by including private and non-concessional flows, new tools of development finance); and results achieved, in order to make positive and negative impacts effectively *measurable* (Severino

DOI: 10.1057/9781137505903.0005

and Ray 2009: 17–20, see also Hynes and Scott 2013: 10–17). In addition, also the *real* role and influence exerted by multilateral organisations both as a whole and as individual agencies should be better reflected. Particularly relevant in this case would be an indication of the proportion between concessional and non-concessional funds channelled by international financial institutions, as these institutions exert a relevant influence upon recipients' countries through *non*-concessional funds (Riddell 2007: 80) and they also act as 'gatekeepers' for the majority of aid flows to sub-Saharan Africa so that countries that do not have an agreement with the World Bank or the International Monetary Fund are extremely unlikely to receive other aid flows (Williams 2000: 567).

Whereas dedicated statistics and data on some of the issues mentioned earlier (for instance on ODA of non-DAC countries) are currently provided by the DAC database, a crucial problem with the ODA is that not only does it not reflect *how* and *how many* resources effectively 'touch the ground' of recipient countries, but it also does not reflect how many leave recipient countries, in the form of repayments on loans, repatriated profit, illicit finance flows[21] or in other, more or less, visible and known ways. Outflows (of different resource types) from recipient countries that may exceed inflows (of different resource types) (EU 2014: 12, see Severino and Ray 2009: 22, Keijzer 2012: 2).

Not only has the ODA been agreed upon by major donors as a *flexible* compromise 'between *political* expediency and *statistical* reality' (Hynes and Scott 2013: 1, emphasis added) but, more importantly, it has also been designed 'by OECD nations to assess OECD nations' (Severino and Ray 2009: 22), not the *impacts* of their actions. In this sense, according to Severino and Ray 'it is hard to find other examples of public policies whose performance is assessed so little on the basis of results and so much on the basis of *expenses* – themselves *measured so imperfectly*' (2009: 16, emphasis added).

As we have already seen, the emphasis on measurement and assessment that inform foreign aid practices is a crucial component of foreign aid governmental strategy. It is related with the ways in which, on the one hand, spaces and technologies of interventions are constructed and governed at all levels as *measurable* and *calculable* ones. On the other hand, it is also related to the fabricated *technical* nature of foreign aid practices that in this way is constantly reinstated. In addition, the pretended measurability of aid also plays a crucial communication role in keeping public attention and constituents alive, and in legitimating the existence and

DOI: 10.1057/9781137505903.0005

role of foreign aid apparatus and experts. It is thus not surprising that a recurrent emphasis is registered in public debate on the 'ideal' *quantity* of aid to be transferred – continuously revived in relation to the 0.7 per cent of GDP global target fixed by the United Nations in 1970, or to the most recent targets fixed within the Millennium Development Goals frame. Calling for renewed efforts, for more coherent commitments to the targets set by the United Nations and by donor states in multiple occasions and settings, provides a self-evident argument to explain why aid has not yet worked as it should have (the so-called aid fatigue). At the same time, it provides an argument as to why it is urgent and necessary to continue to give.

More crucially, the emphasis on ODA is a crucial element for the working of the foreign aid regime as a *moral activity* (Dean 2010: 19), not only in relation to recipient countries and populations, but also by allowing the visibility of donors' self-regulating, self-governing capacities and concerns. In this sense, as preciously highlighted by Hattori, the DAC acts as the contemporary 'moral bookkeeper' of foreign aid practices, thus replacing the role played by religious authorities in ancient religious gift-giving practices (Hattori 2003: 236). The DAC has in fact asserted itself as 'the authenticator of foreign aid as a virtuous practice' by means of its annual statistical reporting and 'peer review' activities on donors' ODA flows; through its continued promotion of multilateral aid against bilateral one; through its routinised praise of good donors and admonishment of bad ones; and through the results it has obtained in promoting the untying of aid[22] and the increase in the proportion of grants to loans (2003: 241, 241–3). In this way, the DAC has constructed those practices which essentially remain bilateral, *qualitative* practices as a *collective* endeavour that is capable of improving and willing to be subject to public scrutiny, promoted by a virtuous and elitist community of states. A virtuous community of states that share common 'good' values, technology and culture in contrast to suspect 'new', 'emerging', 'non-DAC' donors that pose a challenge to 'Western ideas of the right sort of giving' (*The Economist* quoted in Gray 2011: 7). Behind (or below) *measurable* ODA, foreign aid practices can thus continue to operate and expand as *qualitative* practices. Behind (or below) ODA and other targets and indicators, each donor 'composes' and allocates its foreign aid flows according to a complex mix of its varied and ever-changing political, economic and geopolitical profile and agenda. Behind (or below) ODA and other targets and indicators, foreign aid *practices*

DOI: 10.1057/9781137505903.0005

variously intermingle with each donor's[23] and the elitist community of 'good' donors' individual and collective financial, trade, investment and strategic policies.

Thus, the quantity of 'generosity' does not say much about the quantity of 'real aid' that is extended. It also does not say much about its quality, about the nature of the gift that is extended. More importantly, it does not say much on the ways in which the gift is *returned*.

The intrinsic logic of foreign aid practices was effectively captured, already at the end of the 1960s, by Tanzanian President Julius Nyerere, who tried to implement a model of self-reliance organised according to the principles of 'African socialism', a form of socialism he named *ujiamaa*.[24] With the aim of urging developing countries to rely upon their forces, to work to promote their 'self-reliance', autonomy and 'autocentred development' (see Rist 2008: 123–34), he lucidly pointed out – in the Arusha Declaration adopted by the Tanganyika African National Union (TANU) on 5 February 1967 – the intrinsic logic of the foreign aid regime. Nyerere's reasoning deserves to be quoted at length:

> It is stupid to rely on money as the major instrument of development when we know only too well that our country is poor. *It is equally stupid, indeed it is even more stupid, for us to imagine that we shall rid ourselves of our poverty through foreign financial assistance rather than our own financial resources.* It is stupid for two reasons.
>
> Firstly, we shall not get the money. It is true that there are countries which can, and which would like to, help us. But there is no country in the world which is prepared to give us gifts or loans, or establish industries, to the extent that we would be able to achieve all our development targets. [...] *But in any case the prosperous nations have not accepted a responsibility to fight world poverty. Even within their own borders poverty still exists, and the rich individuals do not willingly give money to the government to help their poor fellow citizens.*
>
> *It is only through taxation,* which people have to pay whether they want to or not, that money can be extracted from the rich in order to help the masses. [...] *And there is no World Government which can tax the prosperous nations in order to help the poor nations; [...]*
>
> Secondly, [...] Even if there was a nation, or nations, prepared to give us all the money we need for our development, *it would be improper for us to accept such assistance without asking ourselves how this would effect our independence and our very survival as a nation. Gifts which increase, or act as a catalyst, to our own efforts are valuable. Gifts which could have the effect of weakening or distorting our own efforts should not be accepted until we have asked ourselves a number of questions.*

DOI: 10.1057/9781137505903.0005

The same applies to *loans. It is true that loans are better than 'free' gifts.* [...]

But even loans have their limitations. *You have to give consideration to the ability to repay.* [...] *To burden the people with big loans, the repayment of which will be beyond their means, is not to help them but to make them suffer. It is even worse when the loans they are asked to repay have not benefited the majority of the people but have only benefited a small minority.*

How about the *enterprises of foreign investors?* [...]

Had we been able to attract investors from America and Europe to come and start all the industries and all the projects of economic development that we need in this country, *could we do so without questioning ourselves?*

Could we agree to leave the economy of our country in the hands of foreigners *who would take the profits back to their countries?* Or supposing they did not insist upon taking their profits away, but decided to reinvest them in Tanzania; could we really accept this situation without asking ourselves what *disadvantages* our nation would suffer? [...]

How can we depend upon gifts, loans, and investments from foreign countries and foreign companies without endangering our independence? The English people have a proverb which says, 'He who pays the piper calls the tune'. How can we depend upon foreign governments and companies for the major part of *our development without giving to those governments and countries a great part of our freedom to act as we please? The truth is that we cannot.* (Nyerere 1967, emphasis added)

Nyerere's project did not succeed. Even though he tried to set various conditions in order to make foreign aid functional to self-reliance, his project faced many internal and external challenges. By 1977, Tanzania's development was heavily reliant on foreign aid up to a ratio of 60 per cent (Rist 2008: 133–4). His analysis however, very perspicuously, problematises the intrinsic and peculiar strategy of the foreign aid regime. Firstly, he highlights that foreign aid interventions, being a peculiar form of gift-giving practices, are aimed at establishing or maintaining *ties, links* and *relationships*. The objective of foreign aid practices, their intrinsic logic, is to 'perpetuate the aid relationship' itself (Gould 2005: 69). It is not their quantitative dimension that matters, but their *quality* – not money in itself, but what money carries with it. Despite their benevolent appearance and appeal, they in fact pose a particularly harsh challenge to *independence*. This is a challenge that should always be questioned and addressed. By exploiting the indeterminate and indeterminable nature of the *intention* of giving, in which various degrees of self-interest and of interest in others multifariously coexist, they effectively perpetuate the

DOI: 10.1057/9781137505903.0005

'double bind' according to which their logic 'seems to be to increase the freedom to stay in a [...] relationship, while yet not having to *exit* from obligations' (Verhezen 2005: 38). They evoke conservation of conflict, externally guided operation and inequality (that is 'they may weaken and distort national efforts') but they also, simultaneously, evoke transformation towards peace, cooperation and equality (that is they may act as 'catalyst' to national efforts). They may favour a more 'developed' independence while at the same time they lock in a certain model of *interdependence*. In a 1949 Message on Point Four Legislation, Truman perfectly expresses the 'double bind' logic of foreign aid practices:

> In the economically under-developed areas of the world today there are new creative energies. We look forward to the time when these countries will be *stronger* and more *independent* than they are now, and *yet more closely bound to us* and to other nations by ties of friendship and commerce, and *by kindred ideals*. (Truman 1949b, emphasis added)

Secondly, foreign aid practices are not aimed at addressing recipient states' *poverty* because, as Nyerere highlights, they are not a form of world *redistribution*. They are the *generous* extension of aid, of help, not an assumption of responsibility. In this sense, they allow the shifting of attention and the responsibility for poverty upon the receiver. It is not the donor of aid that is attempting to help out of generosity to be deemed responsible for poverty, but rather the receiver that is incapable of making good use of such help. Through this logical and 'practical' sleight of hand, poverty and 'underdevelopment' causes are *displaced* from outside, from the quality of *interdependence* (international, *structural* constraints) to inside, to the quality of *independence* (recipient countries' domestic, *internal* constraints). Material inequality is constructed as deriving from a set of domestic, technical limitations, and no longer visible as also connected to structural, past and current international power relations. It is constructed as a problem of *internal* capacity (see previous sections).

This intrinsic logic is further reinforced by the construction of foreign aid practices as *unilateral, unreciprocated* gift-giving practices. This is made possible, firstly, because despite the name 'aid' or 'assistance', a proportion of ODA comes in the form of loans, and thus it generates a financial, real *debt* that makes recipient countries materially and discursively visible for their *indebtedness* (Hattori 2003: 233). Secondly, foreign aid practices are made *visible* as unreciprocated practices because recipient countries' counter-giving, through policy conditionality and in many other forms, is not made *visible* as a form of reciprocation, and thus it is always perceived as insufficient. Their debt cannot be settled even though it requires continuous, varied and ever-expanding 'counter-giving'. Just as the German word for debt (*schuld*) means both 'debt' and 'fault', recipient countries' debt matters as much in its concrete, financial terms as in its 'moral' ones. It is at the same time a debt and a guilt-ridden fault. Their lack of development is a debt and guilt-ridden fault, an intrinsically *impossible-to-settle debt* and an *impossible-to-expiate guilt*. Foreign aid relationships have made North–South relations governable by constructing them as relations based on *debt*. They have made recipient countries and populations visible and governable for their material, but also cultural and moral, *indebtedness*; for their substantial *untrustworthiness*. For their continuously renovated and ever-changing *debt* of development.

Thirdly, as Nyerere highlights, foreign aid gift should be questioned because it is the expression of a sophisticated *defensive, conservative* strategy. In yet another intervention on the matter, namely in his 1951 Letter to the Chairman of the International Development Advisory Board, Truman clearly states:

> The Point IV concept, properly carried out, is essential to the successful defense of the free world. In the words of your report, 'strengthening the economies of the underdeveloped regions and an improvement in their living levels must be considered a vital part of our own *defense mobilization*'. [...]
>
> *The building of military strength is not enough to win the peace we seek.* We must press the attack in the battle of raising the living standards and fulfilling the *hopes of mankind for a better future.* (Truman 1951, emphasis added)

Whereas in Truman's letter security and defense aims are still intended in their traditional, cold-war rivalry terms, his writing is however useful to highlight that foreign aid practices could not operate their *defensive, conservative* function without continuously activating the intrinsic *transformative* potential that they, differently from any other traditional economic, strategic practices, bring forward. It is, at the same time, the conservation of the 'free' world and the fulfilling of 'the hopes of mankind' that is at stake. Or better, the defence of the 'free' world is possible by making appeal to the excessive nature of gift/aid, to its relating to 'a hope, a sigh, a dream for what is not yet and [*yet*] can never be given' (Verhezen 2005: 119). As the ideal of the 'free gift' is always present in the

DOI: 10.1057/9781137505903.0005

practice of gift, the ideal of *transformative* foreign aid, of the possibility to redress the *present* and to move towards the *future,* is intrinsic to foreign aid practices. The hope they carry is always present, their transformative effects are *always-to-come.* What is continuously given through foreign aid resources is the possibility to change, to ameliorate, to open a new space, to redress inequality and re-orient interdependence. In much the same way as a gift has value, even though it does not come with the price tag, foreign aid's most important value, *hope,* is priceless but it has *costs.*

Fourthly, loans are better than gifts, as Nyerere says, because foreign aid just like the proper 'traditional' Maussian gift generates a debt that calls for a return action, in both material terms but also, crucially, in terms of *gratitude* and *recognition* of the donor's status. As a proper 'traditional' Maussian gift, it is a channel of the donors' identity and way of life. However, in contrast to a Maussian gift, the foreign aid gift does not imply the *recognition* of recipients' identity. It does not leave any space for recipients' identities, models and values. It is constructed as a *gracious* gift that aims at reshaping recipient countries and populations' identity. But, in contrast to a 'traditional' *gracious* gift, foreign aid gift is not unilateral because it comes with clear expectations of reciproca-tion in both a *simultaneous* and *time-deferred* manner (see Chapter 1 and previous sections). This new form of gift is therefore the perfect, not apparently exploitative, coercive or violent, extension of Western countries' long history of alleged 'cultural', economic and political supe-riority, of centuries of varied 'civilising missions'. Exceeding the formal, established, *visible* rules of other forms of exchange, its level of intrusion is, as Nyerere emphasises, far more dangerous and threatening. It more easily penetrates into the recipient country's 'identity' and it undermines it in a peculiar fashion and puts it into question. The *debt* it produces is also a debt of *civilisation* and *culture.* The related costs are also identity, civilisational and cultural costs (see Latouche 2005: 89–94).

In order to adequately operate their governmental function, foreign aid practices need to be distinctively *visible* and *communicable* and as such *nameable.* In a then confidential document prepared in 1951 by the National Security Council Staff of the United States it is made clear that Point Four has to remain, at least in public perception, distinct from any other foreign programme, such as military, strategic and defence programmes, economic and trade policies or other programmes more limited in time and extent. Otherwise, it is said, 'it would lose much of its *political* and *psychological* effectiveness and be looked upon with

DOI: 10.1057/9781137505903.0005

suspicion as a cloak for colonialism' (National Security Council Staff 1951: 1654, emphasis added). Whereas foreign aid practices have been designed to work in close connection with other international governmental programmes, and the promotion of 'coherence' between these programmes and aid is currently high on the agenda of donors (Keijzer 2012), they can deploy their conservative/defensive potential and maintain their 'hope after hope' vocation, as long as they are perceived as *distinct* and *separated* from other traditional foreign practices. They can operate as long as they are visible in quantitative terms and much less for their intrinsic *quality*.

Notes

1   In a number of passages of his speech Truman explicitly positions the United States 'ahead of its time', see Truman (1949a: 7, 23–9).
2   For a broad and effective analysis of the different conceptualisations of the idea of development in Western thought, see Rist (2008).
3   As brilliantly highlighted by Veca, any notion of difference, of diversity, presupposes that there is something that is *identical*, that does not vary. Otherwise, lacking a common invariable element, or set of elements, two realities would be incommensurable the one with the other, radically others, 'untranslatable' (Veca 1981: x).
4   This section draws inspiration from Riddell (2007), Rist (2008) and Eggen and Roland (2014). See these writings for a more detailed analysis of development theories, programmes and strategies.
5   The Pearson Report's official title was *Partners in Development. Report of the Commission on International Development*, and it had been commissioned by the newly appointed President of the World Bank, Robert McNamara, to a commission headed by Lester B. Pearson.
6   For an overview of the many official institutional reports that were elaborated over the years, see Riddell (2007), Rist (2008) and Eggen and Roland (2014).
7   The PRSPs are also constructed as 'softer' because a lot of emphasis is placed on flexible, 'soft' conditions such as structural benchmarks and other monitoring tools (Lie 2005: 6, Anders 2005: 51–2). Anders has highlighted how in spite of the emphasis on 'soft' conditions the PRSPs do not dismiss 'hard' conditions, and the combination of soft and hard conditionality has created a 'considerable increase of conditions' to be respected (2005: 52). The difference between hard and soft conditions is also the fact that the first type of conditionality mainly operated *ex post*, whereas the second operates *ex ante* (Lie 2005: 13).

DOI: 10.1057/9781137505903.0005

8   According to Dean, the 'technologies of agency' and the 'technologies of performance' are important components of the rationalities, technologies and practices of the different forms of 'advanced liberal government' that constitute the ways of governing in contemporary liberal democracies. Dean, following Rose, articulates the difference between neoliberalism and advanced liberalism and this can be found in Dean (2010: 175–203).

9   For the analysis of the proposals, actors and approach of the Stockholm Initiative, see Van Gastel and Nuijten (2005).

10   A very basic and extremely limited list of variously oriented bibliographical sources on these approaches includes: on human development, Nussbaum and Sen (1993), Sen (1999), Alkire (2002), Fukuda-Parr (2003); on the relations between development and human rights Tomasevski (1993), Eade (1998), Slim (1995, 2002); on human security, Duffield (2001a, 2007) and Larzillière (2012); for a short analysis of the different stances put forward by each of them, Gasper (2007).

11   In this light, for instance, the European Commission has recently called for enhanced links between private and public finance (EU 2014: 16). For the analysis of the ways in which 'development management' technology has absorbed and integrated the 'New Public Management' performance agenda which emerged in the 1980s in Northern countries, see Duffield (2001a) and Brinkerhoff (2008).

12   The UN Global Compact initiative aims at developing strategic partnerships with private companies that are committed to aligning their operations and strategies with ten principles in the area of 'human rights, labour, environment and anti-corruption'. See the website of the initiative at: https://www.unglobalcompact.org, date accessed 15 September 2014.

13   For a detailed picture on multilateral organisations, see Riddell (2007), Stokke (2009).

14   In a recent research Kuziemko and Werker (2006) highlight that when a recipient country is a rotating member of the United Nations Security Council the share of aid it receives from the United States, both directly and through a UN agency, increases respectively by 59 per cent and by 8 per cent, and even more consistently when its vote is needed for purposes and decisions that are particularly critical for the United States. In this sense, the authors suggest, aid works as a bribe.

15   From a recent survey quoted by Severino and Ray, it emerges, for instance, that Cambodia receives an average 400 missions by donors per year, Nicaragua 289 missions, whereas Bangladesh 250. They also highlight that as overall cash transfers to recipient countries have not significantly increased over the years, the proliferation of actors implies that the size of funded projects has decreased sharply (2009: 6).

DOI: 10.1057/9781137505903.0005

16 The need to base North–South relations on fair, contract-based trade relations along with or as a substitute for foreign aid is a recurrent theme in the debate on foreign aid. The focus on business relationships informed by pragmatic mutual interest is also one of the main differences between the Beijing model and the donor-centred Western one: see Eggen and Roland (2014: 94).

17 Gozzi has for instance pointed out that the language of human rights has been adopted and increasingly re-interpreted by Third World social movements to substantiate their resistance, opposition and political–cultural fight against developed countries' development policies and universalist ideology (Gozzi 2010: 374–8, see also Black 2004: 127–42).

18 The DAC List of ODA Recipient countries is available at: http://www.oecd.org/development/stats/daclistofodarecipients.htm, date accessed 6 October 2014.

19 For the definition and for further details on ODA eligibility criteria, see OECD (2008).

20 For the interesting investigation, informed by the adoption of gift theory insights, of China's and India's construction of 'foreign aid' within South–South relationships, see Mawdsley (2012). For an analysis conducted from the same perspective in relation to Russia as a 'new donor', see Gray (2011).

21 In 2013 a group of civil society organisations launched at European level a campaign against tax-related capital flight aptly entitled *Giving with one hand and taking with other*. For more information see: http://www.eurodad.org/takingwithonehand2013, date accessed 28 October 2014.

22 See for instance the many DAC Recommendations on Untying ODA that are available at: http://www.oecd.org/development/untyingaidtherighttochoose.htm, date accessed 15 September 2014.

23 For the analysis of foreign aid policies of different donors, see Stokke (1989), Lancaster (2007) and Veen (2011).

24 *Ujamaa* is a Swahili word that literally means 'family-hood' and it was chosen to emphasise the African-ness of the policies to be adopted (Rist 2008: 129, footnote 21).

DOI: 10.1057/9781137505903.0005

3
Dis/Ordering the World

Abstract: *This chapter investigates in which ways the notion of sovereignty together with its shifting conceptions form part of the foreign aid regime governmental rationality. Distinguishing between the conservative/conflictual and the transformative/cooperative potential intrinsic to any gift-giving practice, Furia then uses these categories to analyse the ways in which foreign aid practices have been interpreted and themes such as poverty, inequality and the obligation to extend aid, have been constructed and put into practice in the operations of the foreign aid regime. In conclusion, the same categories are applied to the notions of community/immunity and order/disorder, to show how the foreign aid regime proliferates through the continuous interplay between the one(s) and the other(s).*

Keywords: global dis/order; global justice; poverty/global inequality; quasi-states; sovereignty

Furia, Annalisa. *The Foreign Aid Regime: Gift-Giving, States and Global Dis/Order.* Basingstoke: Palgrave Macmillan, 2015. DOI: 10.1057/9781137505903.0006.

DOI: 10.1057/9781137505903.0006

What started as a regime of international government of North–South relations, the foreign aid regime has over the years rapidly expanded to a regime of government of recipient countries and of selected groups of population within and across them. Whereas the affirmation of the principle of equal *sovereignty* is one of the conditions that have made possible the establishment of the foreign aid regime, its expansion has been nurtured by the ways in which the notion of sovereignty has been increasingly revised in order to allow, as in the nineteenth century, for a differentiation amongst states in the international domain. On the one hand, the equal sovereignty of all states is the condition that makes it possible to present foreign aid interventions as *technical* interventions, as interventions promoted by '*specialised* agencies with a limited mandate in relation to a sovereign state' (Anders 2005: 47). On the other, the foreign aid regime has proliferated upon the ways in which the notion of *sovereignty* has been reconceptualised in international theory and practice. In addition, the foreign aid regime has contributed in a peculiar way to pave the way to this conceptual shift. Foreign aid interventions contribute to fragment recipient states' space of sovereignty through their 'networked' form of governmental rationality, and their territorial and non-territorial forms of interference and interaction (Duffield 2002: 1062). But they can do so because they have been increasingly entrusted with the task of enabling recipient states to resume or enhance the 'quality' of their (domestic) sovereignty and relations.

The intrinsically ambiguous nature of foreign aid practices also translates into the elaboration of ambivalent notions of order and international community, which can be analysed by drawing from reflections on gift-giving practices. In literature, the inherent ambivalence of gift practice has given rise to two main, divergent interpretations. The first one focuses attention on gift-giving's *conflictual* potential of domination and appropriation, on its being related to the affirmation of superiority and hierarchy and thus on the *conservation of distance* between actors. According to the second one, the extension of a gift is a gesture, a practice that carries with it a *transformative* potential for it aims at promoting cooperation and reciprocal recognition, at *reducing distance* between the giver and the receiver, and therefore at creating a new space of interaction. When the extension of a gift takes place in a context of inequality, as in the case of the foreign aid gift, the question of the conservation or reduction of distance becomes critical and even more ambiguous.

DOI: 10.1057/9781137505903.0006

In the context of the first, *conflictual* interpretative domain, according to Bourdieu, the givers are always moved by the desire to display their power and ability through the extension of a gift. In such an exchange, even between unequals there is however space for the recognition of a form of equality:

> In even the most *equal* gift, the virtuality of the effect of domination exists. And the most *unequal* gift implies, despite everything, an act of exchange, a *symbolic act of the recognition of equality in humanity* [...]. (1998:100, emphasis added)

According to the second, *cooperative* interpretative line, the extension of a gift can be seen as an expression of solidarity, a form of sharing because the givers share what they have with the receivers, a practice that Hénaff terms *solidarity-based gift-giving* (see Chapter 1). Whereas according to Hénaff the aim of this practice is to help and support those who are in *need* and to respond to scarcity (2010c), according to Verhezen a form of sharing and solidarity 'is more likely to be perceived in relationships between equals than among unequals' (2005: 61).

Along with that of *equality/inequality*, the question of *recognition* is particularly critical to gift-giving practices in that it relates to the interpretation of gift-giving as a tool to promote the creation of a *community* (of a new order) or rather as an expression of an already existing one. Whereas the intent to (somehow) recognise and to be recognised is intrinsic to the dynamic of reciprocity inherent in gift-giving practices, the question as to whether this dynamic is the expression of an already existing communal bond or whether it provides in itself grounds for its creation, is open to debate (Osteen 2002: 5). In the context of foreign aid practices, the investigation of such dense 'poles', *equality/inequality*, *recognition/misrecognition* and *expression/creation* of a *community*, obviously needs to be mediated by considering the ways in which the notion of *sovereignty* is conceived. It is in this light that this chapter further investigates, from an international perspective, some of the dimensions already addressed in the previous one. The first and the second sections further scrutinise the operations of the foreign aid regime by analysing theoretical contributions and practices that allow the respective problematisation of those which I term as the conflictual/conservative potential and the cooperative/transformative potential of foreign aid practices. Both those sections link the critical analysis of foreign aid practices' ambivalent potential with the investigation of the role that is played by the theme of poverty in opposition to that of inequality, as well

DOI: 10.1057/9781137505903.0006

as by the conceptualisation and 'practice' of sovereignty. The final section complements the analysis by putting into play Esposito's concepts of *communitas* and *immunitas* and the notions of 'order/disorder' to show how the foreign aid regime proliferates through the continuous interplay between the one(s) and the other(s). Again, even though they are analysed separately, all the aspects addressed in the different sections are to be intended as closely interlinked.

Conflict, poverty and quasi-states

> *Timeo Danaos et dona ferentes.*
> (*Virgil, Aeneid, II:49*)

Investigating what I call the *conflictual/conservative* impact of foreign aid practices gives the possibility to identify the many dimensions and directions along which such gift-giving practices peculiarly contribute to reinforce and shape the *distance* between donor and recipient countries. The ways in which development truth, knowledge and discourse construct and represent developing countries, which have been already investigated in detail in Chapter 2, can be summed up, as Naz suggests, under the headings '*fear, absences*, and *hierarchies*' (2006: 74). Closely interlinked and yet operating at diverse levels, they produce *ahistorical* representations of Third World countries and populations as actors to be looked at with suspicion and fear, as an ever-changing, uniform and almost indifferently spread, collection of gaps, 'handicaps', abnormalities and potential *threats*. They are therefore conceptualised through a series of *absences* – from the lack of modernisation, growth and technical knowledge, to the lack of human rights, capabilities and good governance, from the lack of rational and efficient behaviour, to the lack of security, resilience and so forth – that wait to be remedied and rectified. Development truth, knowledge and discourse produce an evolutionary *hierarchisation* based on the 'normative expectation' for 'underdeveloped' countries to evolve into developed ones (2006: 76). Constructing assumptions on developed countries' historical paths, cultural and behavioural norms, economic structure and technological assets, political and social traditions and environmental practices as the (individual and collective) parameters of *equality*, they represent developing countries as individually and collectively *unequal*.

DOI: 10.1057/9781137505903.0006

The ways in which inequality, and thus equality, is produced have been differently problematised by dependency, world system theories and at a later stage by the post-structural and postcolonial development critique, and obviously in varied ways within each school of thought. In this rich and broad field,[1] postcolonial and post-structural theorists mainly focus on *cultural, discursive* and *representational* construction of inequality, whereas dependency and world system ones predominantly focus on its *material, historical,* namely *political* and *economic,* construction. These theoretical perspectives are obviously far more dense and wide ranging than presented here. However by critically approaching their basic assumptions one can single out at least two, amongst others, ways in which the foreign aid gift further contributes to the construction and positioning of developed and developing countries' identity and inequality.[2] By adopting a post-structural/postcolonial point of view what clearly emerges is that developing countries (and populations) are historically, discursively and culturally constructed as *unequals* due to the production of binary, monolithic categorisations and totalising narratives that allow, on the one hand, to subordinate and dominate their *differences;* on the other, to entrap these differences (together with their diversity and multiplicity) into form, logic and postulations that do not allow them to be *visible, speakable* and *recognised* as worthy (Sidaway 2008, Kapoor 2008).

Adopting a dependency point of view, on the other hand, helps to highlight that developing countries (and populations) are maintained and 'condemned' to *inequality* also due to the perpetuation of international *unequal* structural, socioeconomic and political conditions and relations operated by Western countries (Kapoor 2008, Rist 2008). Shadowing such complex and crucial dynamics, development truth, knowledge and discourse construct developing states' *inequality* mainly as a problem of (lack of) *development.* A problem that thus needs to be measured and addressed according to development epistemology, narrative, technical tools and various metrics. Secondly, they construct developing states' inequality as an *individual, ahistorical* and *depoliticised* issue for the production of which no role is attributed to developed states' historical, economic and political *responsibility.*

Upon this already complicated and very powerful construction of *intuitive, self-evident, natural* identities, foreign aid practices as giving practices add yet another layer. Not only are developed countries rational, modern, independent, active, skilled countries in relation to irrational,

DOI: 10.1057/9781137505903.0006

archaic, subaltern, passive, untalented ones. Not only are they wealthy, cultured, advanced and enlightened countries in relation to destitute, illiterate, backward and 'obscure' ones. Not only are they developed and thus the only possible 'developers' of countries that need to be developed (see Cowen and Shenton 1996). They are also *donors*. Their superior, privileged status compels them, casts on them the burden of helping the less fortunate out of their *good conscience, moral values* and *benevolent attitude*, or *enlightened self-interest*. By voluntarily giving foreign aid they can show off, they can make *visible*, through proper public ceremonies and fanfare, through 'flags on grain sacks, insignias on equipment, sponsor name on NGO literature', their *generosity* and *vitality* (Kapoor 2008: 87, Aaltola 1999: 379). As emphasised by Kapoor and Silva, their national *unity* and *honour* are built (and rebuilt) in a powerful, embellished narrative that revolves around the obligation to help and allows them to perform their 'historical catharsis' (Silva 2008: 24, see Kapoor 2008: 86). Through giving, they extend their sovereignty beyond their territorial borders and thus increase their 'sovereignty and viability' at international level (Aaltola 1999: 379); they become 'generous nations' (Kapoor 2008: 86). Being a culturally and historically constructed practice, foreign aid-giving is an expression of the donor's identity that calls for recognition, respect, gratitude and even envy (2008: 87). It is an act that carries with it the donor's moral values and possible religious meanings, together with varying and various notions of solidarity, humanitarianism, good deeds and charity (2008: 79). Based on post-structural insights, the extension of foreign aid gift, although predominantly framed as a material practice, should thus also be seen as a discursive/representational practice that is based on the donor's moral and cultural norms, religious attitude and traditions, particular language and rhetoric, and 'universal' normative truths. Drawing on analysis proffered by dependent theory should help, on the other hand, to address the link between foreign aid practices and the structurally unequal context within which foreign aid gift is materially given.

In this sense, it has been for instance argued by Nederveen Pieterse that in development truth, discourse and knowledge material inequality between and amongst states is not framed as such but rather as a matter of *poverty* (2002:1027). Whereas in developed countries domestic poverty is not intended and managed as a matter of development, in the foreign aid regime of truth it becomes a matter to be spelled out and addressed according to development epistemology and narrative. In this context,

DOI: 10.1057/9781137505903.0006

recipient countries' diverse and different forms of *richness* are not made *visible*, are disregarded as intrinsically worthless or as detrimental to development (see Sidaway 2008, Latouche 2005). Secondly, their poverty is framed as a *technical* matter and not also as a matter of international power relations. It is analysed and measured by abstracting from attention to *structural* conditions, from the role played by *rich* countries (Nederveen Pieterse 2002:1027). Although a politically dense and tense issue in the domestic domain, in the international one poverty becomes a *technical*, 'safe' theme (2002: 1027). It is a safe theme because, as Nederveen Pieterse further argues, it is *distant*, it is concentrated in distant countries and it has dramatic effects on distant populations. The causes of poverty are thus deemed to pertain mainly to those countries and populations' insufficient economic development, low level of GDP per capita, various internal adverse (cultural, behavioural, institutional, political) conditions and gaps, whereas complex dynamics of global inequality which also have an effect on internal dynamics are very rarely, or mainly derivatively, problematised (see Nederveen Pieterse 2002, Sen 1999).

Through the prioritisation of the theme of poverty, recipient countries (and populations) are thus recognised as *equals* because they are members, to quote Truman's words, of the 'human family', but they are the (in multiple ways distant) *poor* members of such a family. The cultural, representational and structural practices that produce their inequality become even more invisible, and even more difficult to acknowledge and to subject to radical problematisations. As domestic poor people, they are seen as *needy, unfortunate, hopeless* and *victims* in need of guidance, education and cultivation; in need of resources and training; in need of help and of assistance, and therefore in need of *aid*. As domestic poor people have been historically seen and investigated in relation to their possibility to become part of 'working classes' or, more worryingly, of 'dangerous classes' (Procacci 1998:17), poor countries (and populations) are offered the chance to become *trustable* as long as they commit to actively comply with donors' models and instructions and as long as they become 'labourers' of the system. At the same time, they need to be conducted because they pose a *threat*, they are potentially *dangerous*; and thus they need to be constantly monitored, observed and classified.

The analogy with the domestic treatment of poverty is also useful to address the theme of *sovereignty*. As already highlighted in Chapter 1, the post-Second World War international community is founded upon the principle of the sovereign equality of states. The complex and wide theme of sovereignty can be usefully addressed within this context by drawing from Simpson's investigation on the matter (see 2004). The value of Simpson's account in relation to this study lies on at least two methodological reasons. Firstly, whereas he takes into account and addresses the insights and perspectives of realist, classical liberal (or legalist) and also of that which Wight terms as 'revolutionist' traditions of international thought (see 1987: 223–6), he very efficaciously propounds an approach in which the notion of sovereignty becomes the 'place' in which the simultaneous operations of those traditions and conceptions may be seen and investigated by focusing on their complex and contradictory results in terms of legal norms, institutions, doctrines and practice[3] (see 2004: 14–15). Secondly, whereas he acknowledges and briefly discusses the main conceptual origins of the idea of sovereign equality and territorial sovereignty, as found in Bodin's, Pufendorf's and Hobbe's theories and in the renewed influence of Stoic thought,[4] he also shows how the traditional image that identifies a shift from pre-Westphalian hierarchy to post-Westphalian sovereign equality needs to be problematised in relation not only to the 'hierarchical' era of imperialism and colonisation but also to the contemporary era of hierarchical distinctions (see 2004: 30–7). As Simpson demonstrates through his impressive historically grounded reconstruction, the international legal order is 'an anarchical system with *constitutional* pretensions to egalitarism but one in which *legal hierarchies* are present, *if muted*' (2004: 67, emphasis added).

In this sense, Simpson argues that the principle of sovereign equality of states refers in its very basic assumptions to the *equality* of states in the sole juridical sphere as it is based on the assumption that states are *unequal* in many other spheres (geographical extension, level of economic productivity, political and constitutional structure and stability, geopolitical position, natural resources) (2004: 39). In this context, equality is thus 'the very essence of sovereignty' for as Simpson explains, 'it makes no sense to claim a state or entity is sovereign if it is in an unequal relationship with another state' (2004: 40). Differently from theories of absolute sovereignty, the principle of sovereign equality as commonly intended is a 'relative sovereignty', in that it is assumed that sovereignty is limited by relationships with other sovereign states and by the same existence of international law (2004: 40–1). Sovereign equality is thus intended as an 'organising principle' that allows the coexistence of states as well as a certain degree of security through immunities and constraints (2004:

DOI: 10.1057/9781137505903.0006

40–1): 'States possess sovereign equality but sovereign equality also operates as a way of structuring their relations' (2004: 41). This founding principle Simpson describes in further detail through the rights and immunities it encompasses, such as the right of self-defence, the right to self-determination, to territorial integrity and to political independence, whose main corollary is the norm of non-intervention (2004: 39–56).

This principle has however always tensely coexisted with various forms of what Simpson names '*legalised hierarchies*' (2004: 62). The two forms of '*legalised hierarchies*' on which Simpson focuses attention in his investigation, whose richness it is not possible to adequately reflect here, offer precious insights for this investigation. Simpson names the first form of hierarchy as '*anti-pluralism*'. This is the practice which emerged in the nineteenth century of subjecting membership (or its quality) in the international community 'to certain *gradation status* based on culture or ideology' (2004: 67, emphasis added), or, as he says in another passage:

> the practice of making legal distinctions between states on the basis of external behaviour or internal characteristics. (2004: xii)

The second form is called 'legalised hegemony', that is a case where 'certain states are accorded a position of pre-eminence or dominance by virtue of their superior 'power' (2004: 67). In particular, Simpson intends 'legalised hegemony', which also emerged in the early nineteenth century, as composed of four elements:

> First, there is a *constitutional or legal basis* to the dominance of certain powers. Their superiority is reflected in *legal norms* and in the *institutions* of particular eras. The phenomenon of legalised hegemony *arises only in the context of an international society*. Second, *there is a form of sovereign equality* existing among the powers themselves (in spite of actual material differences existing between these powers). Third, the directorate of Great Powers[5] acts in concert to achieve certain ends within the international order. These powers *have an interest in* and *prerogatives over*, not only their own narrowly defined interests, *but over the whole international system*. Fourth, legalised hegemony is both *imposed* from above by the Great Powers and also *accepted by consent* from below by the other powers within the system. (2004: 67–8, emphasis added)

Carefully reconstructing the long, confrontational debate amongst diplomats and jurists that led to the adoption of the Charter of the United Nations (San Francisco, 1945) (see 2004: 254–63), Simpson shows that the model produced by the Great Powers with the adoption of the Charter was based on the compromise between 'legislative equality' and

DOI: 10.1057/9781137505903.0006

'legalised hegemony'. 'Legislative equality' is reflected in the composi-
tion of the General Assembly and in some of its powers, and 'legalised
hegemony' is granted by the membership, governing principles and
powers of the Security Council (2004: 179–93). Historically based on the
troubled coexistence between equality and hegemony, the international
order that was created in San Francisco thus reflected, as Simpson points
out, the adaptation of the sovereign equality of all states to the preroga-
tives of the most powerful amongst them (2004: 192–3).

In terms of membership in the international community, alongside
and after the 'original Members', the Charter of San Francisco envisaged
an admission policy according to which 'Membership in the United
Nations is open to all other peace-loving states' (UN 1945: arts. 3 and 4).
As Simpson argues, by agreeing not to add any further specifications to
the adjective 'peace-loving', or to include any other cultural and political
standards, the founders of the United Nations designed a predominantly
'pluralist' model of international community which was based on the
rejection, in the name of the principle of non-intervention, of the 'standard of civilisation' model that informed nineteenth century international
law and of the Holy Alliance interventionist approach (2004: 269).

Particularly since the adoption of the *Declaration on the Granting of
Independence to Colonial Countries and Peoples* (1960), the so-designed
pluralistic admission policy allowed to extend membership to decolo-
nised territories on the basis of a right of self-determination intended
as 'the right held by the majority within a colonially defined territory
to external independence from colonial domination by metropolitan
powers alien to the continent' (2004: 275). This right to self-determination was not granted to ethnic groups living within these territories
or to majorities oppressed by 'indigenous "alien"' elites (2004: 275). It
did not include democratic representation and secession as constitutive
elements and it was based on the idea that these new states were to be
treated *equally*, regardless to 'standards of democracy or constitutional
viability'[6] (2004: 275). As Simpson further notes:

> Sovereignty (now accorded the majority of former colonies), full member-
> ship and statehood were regarded as co-extensive rights of former colonial
> peoples. All states, *rich* and *poor*, were *fully sovereign*. (2004: 275, emphasis
> added)

Along with being increasingly included in an international community
based on the coexistence of sovereign equality and 'legalised hegemony',

DOI: 10.1057/9781137505903.0006

developing states obviously remained unequal from a *material* point of view. They remained *the poor* members of such a community.

In relation to this historical process, Jackson for instance, strongly criticises the framework elaborated in San Francisco for 'repudiating' the older structure and producing a 'negative sovereignty' game that stands in sharp contrast to the 'positive sovereignty' game that emerged in modern Europe and was expressed by Western imperialism and colonialism (1990: 1). In particular, he strongly criticises the peculiar set of rights and the special status that was attributed to Third World countries, which he terms 'quasi-states', in the name of what he defines as 'categorical self-determination' (1990: 41). In contrast to the traditional and more demanding *competitive* game in which sovereignty, and thus the right to self-determination, was a '*historical* right', which was 'demonstrated', merited and gained in the battlefield, the limitation of the new regime is to be found, he argues, in the fact that within it self-determination is no longer seen as 'a positive right of *national* self-determination' but rather as the 'negative right of ex-European colonies [...] to constitutional independence under an indigenous government regardless of conditions or circumstances' (1990: 41, 34–40). Even more disputable according to Jackson is the fact that, besides being attributed independence 'as a matter of right', without earning it in history, 'quasi-states' have enjoyed not only the negative entitlements related to it, such as the right of non-intervention, but have also been attributed, due to their *domestic* incapability and inadequateness, unprecedented *positive* entitlements, such as material support through foreign aid and development assistance (1990: 42–3). The problem with the international development regime is that according to Jackson the differentiation of sovereign states 'in terms of development and underdevelopment' has changed the practice and theory of international relations (1990: 111). On the one hand, 'sovereignty and development have been divorced largely as a result of decolonization' (1990: 111). On the other, development has become 'an international expectation or goal' so that underdevelopment is no longer considered as a problem of the underdeveloped countries themselves but, at least in part, also as a problem 'of the international community and particularly its richest members' (1990: 111). In this context, Jackson for instance describes, in relation to the 'destitute image' of Third World countries, foreign aid interventions as the result of the fact that 'Third World states *advertise* their poverty' to obtain assistance from the international community's richest members. He adds that the latter accept to extend aid because, firstly, aid is deemed to be 'a badge of good citizenship' related to what is believed to be a moral or legal obligation and, secondly, because it is a useful tool for rich countries to promote 'their standing among poor clienteles' (1990: 111–12, 191 emphasis added). It is through this way of thinking that the international society has been transformed from simply being a 'civil association for all states' into being in addition 'a joint enterprise association' that assists its poorer members on a non-reciprocal basis (1990: 48). In the *cooperative* game thus established, foreign aid practices work as a form of 'affirmative action' that attempt, Jackson says, not very successfully to 'compensate for the shortage of positive sovereignty of quasi-states', to reduce the gap between incompetent, corrupt and sometimes abusive 'quasi-states' and 'highly capable and relatively civil states' (1990: 31, 30). Highlighting how the process of 'precipitous decolonization' (1990: 98) and of admission as *equals* in the international community have been based on the neglect of the 'huge differences in talent, skill, experience, discipline, dedication, training, education, perseverance, equipment, opportunities' that inevitably discriminate between 'national popula-tions' (1990: 199), Jackson emphasises that the provision of 'international recognition, dignity, and independence to all colonized populations' has been in many cases exploited by their governments to deny and violate those populations' human rights (1990: 202). In relation to this, Jackson complains that the 'conservatism' of international society has made 'impossible' and 'unthinkable' the effective reconfiguration of the current situation through the establishment of 'alternative arrangements which could supply greater *expertise, responsibility*, and *probity* in government decision-making', particularly in upholding human rights and promot-ing socioeconomic development (1990: 190–1, emphasis added).

Noticing that only some Third World countries would ' "gradu-ate" from the nonreciprocal development regime' that is at work, the alternative arrangements Jackson expresses support for, and thus the 'progressism' he advocates for, would in fact require to overcome the deeply rooted principle of sovereign equality and the corollary principle of non-intervention in the direction of 'trusteeship' (1990: 191). For, he concludes, 'a greater variety of international statuses including more *intrusive* forms of international trusteeship might have rendered the post-colonial situation less unsatisfactory' (1990: 202, emphasis added).

The argumentations expressed by Jackson resonate well with the shift and renewed challenges to the principle of sovereign equality and the

DOI: 10.1057/9781137505903.0006

related principle of non-intervention that have increasingly occurred after the end of the Cold War, and whose broad outlines can be at least mentioned by drawing again from Simpson's analysis. Simpson describes this shift by emphasising that it can be understood as a specific form of 'liberal anti-pluralism'. A descendant of preceding forms of 'anti-pluralism' that emerged in the early nineteenth century and that made possible to distinguish between European nations and non-European semi-sovereigns, 'unequal' or 'uncivilised' states (2004: 20–1), this new form of 'liberal anti-pluralism' has thus increasingly challenged the 'pluralistic' model designed in San Francisco by going back to the idea that it is necessary to distinguish between states depending on their *domestic*, internal characteristics (2004: 80). As Simpson further argues, in the post-Cold War scenario 'liberal anti-pluralism' was revived in international law thinking and to varying degrees in the behaviour and practices of the international community mainly through the construction of two regimes based on two distinct categorisation of states. On the one hand, that which he terms as the *criminal law regime* has increasingly assigned criminal liability to states for 'gross breaches of international law' and has increasingly produced a differentiation between 'legitimate', 'good standing' states and 'terrorist' or 'outlaw' ones, such as aggressive or genocidal ones (2004: 280). On the other hand, the regime that he names as *democratic governance regime* has progressively introduced a differentiation between 'undemocratic', 'illiberal' or 'uncivilised' states – which are the states that, without necessarily being criminal states, violate human rights principles and democratic norms – and 'liberal' ones (2004: 281).

Simpson highlights how in the context of these regimes, theoretical debate and international practices revolve around the definition and legitimacy of varied, and obviously different in every regime, forms of intervention and intrusion – from humanitarian intervention, supervision and forms of engagement, to sanctions, surveillance, 'disciplinary', 'community-sanctioned violence' and military actions (see 2004: 284–99, 299–311) – that expand the sphere of regulation of international law or make it more pervasive. Simpson himself briefly notes that the closely interlinked category of 'failed' states should be added to those categories and regimes related to *inequality*. The specificity of 'failed' states in relation to the other categories of unequal states is however, according to Simpson, that they are *unequal* or, as Jackson would say, 'quasi-states' 'not because of what they do but rather by virtue of *what they are unable to do*' (2004: 281, footnote 10, emphasis added).

DOI: 10.1057/9781137505903.0006

The specific assumption upon which these categories of states are made possible and 'thinkable' is that sovereignty can no longer be conceived as 'a right' but rather it has to be conceived as 'responsibility'.

As it is widely known, in Western political thought and history, since the American and French Revolutions and as a result of a process that had started a long time before, sovereignty was increasingly displaced from the person of the sovereign to the people, the nation.[7] It is with the democratisation of sovereignty, with the affirmation of the sovereignty of the people, that the concept of sovereignty was 'limited' and linked to the achievement of universal, normative goals (human rights), the setting up of the related political, institutional, economic and social arrangements, and the (ideal) notions of *responsibility* and *accountability* (Williams 2000: 563–5, see Dean 2007: 144–5). The tragedy of the Holocaust, the affirmation of human rights principles together with a complex assemblage of other events have increasingly led, since the end of the Second World War and more strongly after the Cold War, to the legal and institutional circumscription of states' *external* and *internal* sovereignty also in the international domain (see Williams 2000, Philpott 2014). Even in international theory and practice, states' sovereignty has thus increasingly become bound up with universal normative assumptions and international obligations (particularly human rights obligations) regarding their *domestic* sphere (Philpott 2014). It has thus come to mean *responsibility* for the population, that is responsibility (and thus capacity) to deliver political goods and services and provide for the basic needs of citizens. And, at a later stage, it has come to mean 'responsibility to protect' citizens from crimes against humanity, genocide, war crimes and ethnic cleansing (Potter 2004).[8] This revised doctrine was for instance expressed in 1992 and in 1998 by the respective United Nations Secretary Generals at the time, Boutros Boutros-Ghali and Kofi Annan, who affirmed that:

> The time of absolute and exclusive sovereignty, however, has passed; its theory was never matched by reality. It is the task of leaders of States today to understand this and to find a balance between the needs of good internal governance and the requirements of an ever more interdependent world. (Boutros-Ghali 1992)

> The Charter protects the sovereignty of peoples. It was never meant as a licence for governments to trample on human rights and human dignity. Sovereignty implies responsibility, not just power. (Annan 1998)

DOI: 10.1057/9781137505903.0006

Not only does the notion of sovereignty as responsibility allow the categorisation of states, but it also allows to redesign sovereignty as a non-absolute and conditional status. In this sense, it confers a responsibility on the international community to determine which states fail to carry out their responsibilities and need assistance or intervention (Potter 2004: 1). In coherence with this shift, 'failed' states have become one of the latest concerns in the theory and practice of the foreign aid regime, as well as one of the latest domains in which its action is expanding and expanded (see Chapter 2).

In this context, pointing to foreign aid's failure in 'saving' failed states and looking for a more 'cost-effective' way to respond to the problems that are raised by 'failed' (or about to fail) states in relation to the promotion of human rights and of international stability (1992–3: 9, 20), Helman and Ratner clearly highlight the link between the intrinsic logic of foreign aid practices and the notion of sovereignty as a conditional status. Firstly, they argue that foreign aid practices *have always been*, for instance by means of conditionality policy (see Chapter 2), *a demonstration of the fact that the theory of equal sovereignty 'was never matched by reality'* (1992–3: 10, emphasis added). Echoing Jackson's reflection, they then propose a system of 'United Nations Conservatorship' that is to be intended as the equivalent of the forms of 'guardianship or trusteeship' that in domestic systems are adopted in response to 'broken families, serious mental or physical illness, or economic destitution' (1992–93: 12). Acknowledging that there is at least an 'irreducible minimum of sovereignty', Helman and Ratner illustrate that such a system would require 'some form of consent of the *host* state', which, depending on circumstances, may range from 'a formal invitation' to 'simply the *absence of opposition'* (1992–3: 13, emphasis added). According to Helman and Ratner's proposal, the United Nations 'guardianship role' would be modelled on past forms of multilateral assistance that need however to be '*modernised'* and oriented towards 'newly non-self-governing territories' by envisaging three models: 'governance assistance', 'delegation of governmental authority' and 'direct U.N. trusteeship'. Each of these models would build upon *existing aid assistance* but 'be far more expansive', and would carry with it an augmented level of intrusion (1992–3: 15, 13). Whereas they propose various practical arrangements and procedures in relation to the management of these forms of 'guardianship' – for instance the creation of an *ad hoc* subgroup within the Security Council with power for initiating and terminating them (see 1992–3:

DOI: 10.1057/9781137505903.0006

18–20) – they emphasise that such forms of 'conservatorship' should be directed to countries whose situation is so 'hopeless' that they 'surrender so much authority to the U.N.', that it should not 'devolve into long-term custody' and that if programmes were to fail the United Nations would 'reassess the state's political viability'[9] (1992–3: 18–19). In relation to the objections their proposal is likely to give birth to, Helman and Ratner assert that arguments based on the respect of 'sovereign equality' are not decisive because sovereignty:

> even as *touted by developing states*, is consistent with the idea of conservatorships because the purpose of conservatorship is to enable the state *to resume responsibility for itself*. (1992–3: 17, emphasis added)

Quite ironically, the (modernised) 'conservatism' propounded by Helman and Ratner is of the same species of the 'progressism' called for by Jackson. That which needs to be 'conserved', or conversely protected in a more 'progressive' way, according to these perspectives, is a space of interdependence that is still made governable by calculating the differences, the *distance* between 'un/equal' sovereigns. As Simpson highlights, the international community continues to be structured around the idea of a 'sovereignty regime in which the *rights and duties of states can vary*' (2004: 321, emphasis added).

Cooperation, friendship and justice

> *Justice is good for peace.*
> (*Isaiah, 32:17*)

Particular to gift-giving practices is the idea, epitomised in Mauss's account, that they represent a *cooperative* form of interaction in contrast with *conflictual* ones, such as war or coercion. Compared to the cooperation established by trade and commerce relations, gift-giving opens the way for forms of interaction that due to their peculiar logic and temporal structure carry with them a more consistent *transformative* potential as they provide the possibility to establish a stable, constantly reproduced and 'personalised' relationship based on reciprocity, recognition and development of trust (see Chapter 1). In addition, being the manifestation 'of the demand for commitment' (Adloff and Mau quoted in Kowalski 2011: 192–3), their main added value in this sense would also

DOI: 10.1057/9781137505903.0006

be to carry with them the potential for moving from (dual) *reciprocity* to (plural) *mutuality* (see Hénaff 2010c: 17–20).

In this context, the analysis of the relationship among gift-giving, friendship and fraternity allows the introduction to some of the many dimensions that are evoked when foreign aid-giving practices are valued for their peculiar *cooperative* and *transformative* potential, for their capacity to reduce distance or to create a new space of relationship. This perspective is reflected in the category of gift-giving Hénaff terms *mutual aid* or *solidarity-based gift-giving* which identifies the field in which Aristotle's *philia* and Weber's *ethic of brotherhood* would operate (see 2010b, 2010c). Whereas Aristotle's and Weber's conceptions have already been briefly investigated in Chapter 1, in this context some precious insights are provided by Hannah Arendt's contribution on the matter.

Drawing inspiration from ancient Greek and Roman ethical thinking, as well as by Lessing's reflection, Arendt in her well-known writing on *Humanity in Dark Times* (which is included in *Men in Dark Times*, 1968) – as well as in other writings such as her equally well-known *On Revolution* (1963) – contrasts the concept of *friendship* with that of *fraternity*. As pointed out by Arendt, Lessing in opposition to his contemporary Rousseau did not find in *compassion*, in the 'innate repugnance [...] to see a fellow human being suffering', the fundamental expression of humanity but rather he thought that true humanity is showed in *friendship*, which is 'as *selective* as compassion is *egalitarian*' (1968[1960]:12, quoting Lessing, emphasis added). Arendt explains that from compassion arises, what Lessing termed as 'philanthropic feelings', a sense of brotherhood with other human beings that springs from revulsion of the world in which human beings are treated 'inhumanly' (1968[1960]: 12–13, quoting Lessing).

Inspired by Rousseau's idea, French revolutionaries, and in particular Robespierre, attempted through compassion 'to achieve solidarity with the unfortunate and the miserable'. As Arendt argues, they transformed fraternity in a political concept, neglecting the fact that fraternity is 'the great privilege of pariah peoples; it is the advantage that the pariahs of this world always and in all circumstances can have over others' (1968[1960]: 14, 13). In doing so, in focusing on such kind of 'humanitarism', they did not understand that this kind of humanitarism 'is not transmissible and cannot be easily *acquired by those who do not belong among the pariahs*'. More critically, they introduced into all modern revolutions the ruinous idea that one should attempt to 'improve the lot of the unfortunate

DOI: 10.1057/9781137505903.0006

rather than *to establish justice for all* (1968[1960]: 14, emphasis added). On the contrary, Arendt, inspired by Lessing, identifies in friendship, in the Greek *philia*, the most precious example of *humanity* (1968[1960]: 25). According to her, compassion has a natural, 'affective nature' but it is 'purely passive' because it makes 'action impossible'; friendship on the other hand relates to a 'humaneness' that is 'sober and cool' and that 'makes *political demands* and preserves *reference to the world*' (1968[1960]: 14–15, 25, emphasis added). The problem with compassion, Arendt highlights in *On Revolution*, is in fact that:

> Compassion [...] *abolishes the distance*, the in-between which always exists in human intercourse [...]. Because compassion abolishes the distance, the *wordly* space between men where *political matters*, the whole realm of human affairs, are located, it remains, *politically speaking irrelevant and without consequence.* (1990[1963]: 86, emphasis added)

Like pleasure and pain, compassion, Arendt emphasises, does not produce speech 'and certainly not *dialogue*'. Compassion happens in 'dark times' when the humanitarianism of brotherhood and the 'warmth' it produces is important as it is the only compensation for the irreality of human relationships developed in absolute 'wordlessness'. Such humanitarism operates in the realm of *invisibility*; it entails the 'loss of the common, *visible* world'. It thus easily leads to conclude that 'the element common to all men *is not the world, but "human nature" of such and such a type*' (1968[1960]: 16, emphasis added). On the contrary, friendship 'humanizes' the world by making the world the object of *dialogue*, of a dialogue between a *plurality* of voices, a dialogue between different *truths*. Arendt affirms in this regard:

> such speech is virtually impossible in solitude; it belongs to an area in which there are many voices and where the announcement of what each 'deems truth' both *links and separates men*, establishing in fact those distances between men which together comprise the world. (1968[1960]: 30–1, emphasis added)

Fraternity due to its *biological* roots relates to *identity* and it produces conflict and hostility against *difference*. As seen in the French revolution, it easily nurtures nationalism, regionalism, localism, ethnocentrism and violence against those who are born of 'different fathers' (Esposito 2006: 66–7, Dovolich 2006). As shown by the Judeo-Christian, Roman and Greek tradition, it is also inherently *fratricidal* (Cain and Abel, Romulus and Remus, Eteocles and Polynices) (Arendt 1990[1963]: 86–8, 208–9, Esposito 2006: 66). Fraternity does not politically produce a new space

DOI: 10.1057/9781137505903.0006

for interaction between differences, it simply obliterates space (and differences), whereas friendship is a *demanding political* concept and goal. There is no friendship (in its political dense sense) without a *public, visible* space for *differences* and without distance. Friendship is not the place for sentimentalism, intimacy, romanticised pity or compassion, but for *solidarity* (see Arendt 1968[1960]: 83–94, Passerin d'Entrèves 1995). It requires *active* openness to the *reality* of the world, to the 'realness' of its reality; 'readiness to share the world with other men' by making it the object of a constant discourse (Arendt 1968[1960]: 22, 25). According to Arendt, pluralistic and reciprocal friendship and solidarity allow for the humanisation of the world, 'are remedies for the reality of human suffering' beyond all forms of hypocrisy, 'moralistic attitudes' and 'pseudoidealistic enterprises' (Owens 2007: 177, note 27, Arendt quoted in 2007: 106).

In the domain opened by the reflections sketched earlier, the exchange of gifts is thus closely related with friendship as it is a means by which distance is accepted (recognised) and at the same time 'transgressed' in order to create the in-between space that nurtures friendship. As Sahlins puts it: *'If friends make gifts, gifts make friends'* (1972: 186, emphasis added).

The intrinsic connection between the extension of the foreign aid gift and the establishment of *friendly* relationship is acknowledged both by political realism and liberal internationalism, and obviously divergently interpreted within the two schools of thought. In very broad terms, whereas for the realist tradition foreign aid is an additional foreign policy tool aimed at establishing or maintaining alliances, and thus at securing power, national interests and security, for the liberal tradition foreign aid is a tool to promote development that contributes to the efforts to enhance equality and cooperation within the international community (Hattori 2001: 634). Within the second perspective, an argument in support of foreign aid comes from the link between the principles of the Charter of the United Nations and of international law, particularly the right to self-determination, and development, which has been affirmed and reaffirmed at the international level through, for instance: the *International Covenant on Economic, Social and Cultural Rights* (1966); the UN 1974 *Declaration on the Establishment of a New International Economic Order* (NIEO); the UN *Declaration on the Right to Development* (1986); the establishment of the Millennium Development Goals (2000); and the 2005 World Summit (see Riddell 2007: 142–53). In this sense,

DOI: 10.1057/9781137505903.0006

according for instance to Bedjaoui, the new post-colonial international community is based on the principle of self-determination to which the right to development, as well as the same existence of the international community, is intrinsically linked:

> The 'open' community of today, which has replaced the 'closed' community of yesterday, owes this distinguishing feature to the self-determination of peoples [...]. Without self-determination there is no contemporary international community [...]. Thus self-determination belongs to the *jus cogens*. The 'right to development' flows from this right to self-determination and is of *the same kind*. For it is pointless to acknowledge self-determination as an overriding and preemptory principle, if we do not simultaneously acknowledge a 'right to development' for the people which has determined its own future. (Bedjaoui quoted in Jackson 1990: 121).

This assumption resonates well with the interpretation, both by recipient countries and populations and some donor agencies, of foreign aid as an *entitlement* to be delivered or requested (Eyben 2005, 2006). In parallel with this perspective, it has been for instance suggested that the continued, official reiteration of donors' commitments to the Millennium Development Goals would render such commitments binding obligations under customary international law (see Riddell 2007: 149–50). The controversy around this interpretation has led to the attempt to extend in practice the discourse on aid as *obligation*. Such as for instance, following a proposal made by Arjun Sengupta (the former UN's Independent Expert on the Right to Development), through the designing of the instrument of 'development compacts'. These are plans of action for the achievement of the Millennium Development Goals agreed upon by recipients and groups of donor countries that are based on the definition of clear objectives, shared responsibilities and reciprocal commitments. Within this framework, in a case in which there would be a lack of adequate resource flows from donors, recipient countries would be in a position to *demand* that donors' commitments be respected (see HDR 2003, Riddell 2007: 150–1). In this context, another way to enhance government's obligations to provide aid would be to extend the 'responsibility to protect' principle to address extreme poverty as a serious form of human rights violation (see Riddell 2007: 151–2 and previous section).

In the same context, but from a different point of view, foreign aid has been interpreted as a form of reparation for past or current wrongs and in this context developing countries would be entitled to receive foreign aid in the name of their *right to reparation*. A paradigmatic example of

DOI: 10.1057/9781137505903.0006

this perspective is represented by the NIEO Declaration.[10] Arguing that developed countries have a duty to transfer resources not as a form of charity or due to obligations of humanity but rather as rectification of past *wrongs*, in the NIEO Declaration developing countries have affirmed the right of states, territories and peoples under 'foreign occupation, alien and colonial domination or apartheid' to 'restitution and full compensation' for the exploitation and depletion of their natural and other resources (UN 1974: point 4, letter f). As highlighted by Opeskin, whereas there is a general consensus that the condition of many developing countries has been affected by colonisation and exploitation, such a perspective poses many scientific difficulties in terms of: the need to differentiate between formerly colonised states and states which were not under colonial domination; the impossibility to verify through a counterfactual assessment how things would have been without foreign domination; the difficulty of identifying who is responsible for the wrongs and who is entitled for reparation, particularly due to the generational turnover; and the determining of the temporal extension of the wrongs and of indebtedness (1996: 26–7). In addition, although the responsibility of developed countries and international institutions in the production and perpetuation of global poverty is asserted by many intellectuals and scholars, far more controversial is the determination of the extent of this responsibility against and in its connection to a multitude of other domestic/local factors (political institutions, ethnic conflicts, inadequate policies, corruption, authoritarian governments, natural resources endowment) (Satz 2005: 48–51).

In the context of his broad analysis on the matter, Jackson describes NIEO Declaration's 'moral logic' and assumption as based on the call for 'a fundamental change of international obligation away from *free trade* and *commutative justice* towards *economic democracy* and *distributive justice*' (1990: 131, emphasis added). In international law, as Simpson highlights, there is in fact no general duty or obligation to produce substantive or economic equality between states as this would be in conflict with states' liberty or sovereignty (2004: 56–7). Whereas the existence of inequalities in the international domain is justified and accepted for the same reasons they are justified and accepted in the domestic domain, it is however possible that states agree upon some policies of redistribution, but, as Simpson further argues, economic sovereignty remains the cornerstone of the system (2004: 58). In addition, the main point is that those egalitarian policies may well spring, as we have already noticed in

DOI: 10.1057/9781137505903.0006

the previous paragraph, not from concerns about *(in)equality* but rather from concerns about phenomena such as absolute or severe material deprivation (2004: 58). As Simpson explains, 'we may agree on closing the gap but disagree profoundly about by how much the gap should be closed' (2004: 58, quoting Schelling). Thus whereas the debate around the possible legal status and possible legal basis for the configuration of a duty to provide aid, or of the related entitlement to aid, is particularly controversial and still open, the idea that such an obligation exists in *moral* terms is commonly held, yet widely debated in relation to its foundations or its beneficiaries.

Beside the ways in which such an idea has variously translated into donors' public justifications of foreign aid and still coexists with charity or altruism narratives (see Riddell 2007: 142–53), the configuration of such a duty has been the object of many ethical reflections resonating well with Hénaff's category of gracious gift-giving, a category within which gift-giving becomes a *moral* practice (see Chapter 1). On the one hand, the introduction of the human needs, human rights-based, human capabilities and human security approaches to development have contributed to the definition of what has been called 'development ethics', an ethical reflection that aims at addressing and discussing the many ethical and moral questions that arise from development theory and practice, such as for instance: the definition of what should count as '(good) development'; the discussion of moral issues that arise in development policymaking and practice; the identification of responsibilities for bringing about development; the distribution of the burdens and benefits of development; and questions related to the 'challenges' posed by 'moral scepticism, *moral relativism, national sovereignty* and political realism' to 'boundary-crossing' ethical inquiry on development (Crocker 2001: 48, 47–9, emphasis added).[11] Some of the reflections developed in relation to the duty to provide aid have increasingly intermingled with those elaborated by 'development ethicists', however the former somehow define an autonomous field whose consideration is useful for this study. It is however a field within which, as highlighted by Nussbaum, a strong consensus is difficult to be reached mainly due to the influence of Cicero's distinction between *iustitia* and *benevolentia*, and thus between universal and binding *duties of justice* and more limited and restrained *duties of material aid* (Nussbaum 2000).[12]

Within this broad and rich field,[13] a first group of scholars and writers, such as Hancock, have argued, adopting a consequentialist point of view,

DOI: 10.1057/9781137505903.0006

that not only is giving aid ineffective because it produces corruption and is ill-managed, but it is also intrinsically *maleficent*, it is *bad* because it causes suffering and miseries, it prevents self-reliance, local initiatives and recognition of recipients' abilities, and its industry is not reformable (1989: 182–3, see Opeskin 1996: 23–4). Conversely, adopting a consequentialist perspective that he terms a 'lifeboat ethics', Hardin (2008) has affirmed that current policies of foreign aid, particularly food aid, are bad not only for developing countries but also for developed ones. Comparing each rich nation to a lifeboat and identifying poor nations with people that swim outside lifeboats, he argues that foreign aid policies should be based on the assumption that each lifeboat has a limited capacity, and thus taking on board more people than the number that would be allowed by considerations of safety would result in the drowning of all (2008: 16–17). Pointing to what he terms as 'the tragedy of the commons' in comparison with a model based on self-responsibility and self-reliance, and to the exhaustion of the environment and the harmful impact on the quality of life of poor people posed by the uncontrolled growth of poor populations sustained by (food) aid, he argues that charitable acts, humanitarian and sharing efforts based on the ideal of pure justice are nothing less than absurd, 'suicidal' and against the interest of posterity (2008: 15, 16, 17–28).

A radically different conclusion is reached by those authors who base their reflection upon those which Opeskin terms as 'obligations of humanity' (1996: 24). In this context, Singer, based on the argument that one is obliged to save a child from drowning if they can do it without too great a cost to them and regardless of whether they have a causal responsibility for the accident, has argued that the same obligation applies in the case of evils that affect *distant* persons. As he explains, if it is in the power of a person to prevent something bad from happening – such as suffering and death because of famine, hunger, lack of medical care – 'without thereby sacrificing anything of comparable moral importance', such person has a *moral obligation* to do it (2008: 3).[14] According to Singer, this obligation is universal as it extends beyond national borders as distance (or proximity) has no *moral significance* in relation to the obligation to provide aid; nor such an obligation is diminished (or reinforced) by the presence (or absence) of other people who could help (2008: 4, see 5–6). As Singer further argues, giving aid is not thus a charitable, generous or 'supererogatory' act but it is a duty for private people. And it should also be crucial to have citizens campaigning for new standards

DOI: 10.1057/9781137505903.0006

for states' public aid, particularly with regard to the need for a greater amount of 'genuine', no-strings-attached aid (2008: 7). Singer adopts a utilitarian perspective and metrics – in that he imposes a requirement to measure the potential benefit of aid in developing countries against the cost to donors in developed ones (2008: 7, 13). Other reflections have elaborated around a duty to material aid within the context of *theories of justice*, particularly of *theories of distributive justice*. In this context, global transfers of resources are justified as a form of global redistribution of wealth (Opeskin 1996: 23). Within this group, as Trujillo argues, ethical theories may interpret material aid as a matter of justice based on a *theory of human rights* or on a *theory of human obligations* (2004: 194). Following Trujillo's argumentation, in the first case divergent interpretations arise depending on the specific theory of rights that is adopted. Whereas for instance within liberal and libertarian theories of rights there are no grounds for a duty to provide aid except out of charity or philanthropy, within 'basic' or 'subsistence' rights theories a duty to provide aid is founded upon the universal nature of such *positive* rights, even though in this case the main difficulty is to identify the subjects who bear the related obligations, provided that developing countries are not able to fulfil them (2004: 196–201). Theories of human obligations, Trujillo highlights, are more likely to overcome the theoretical limitations of human rights approaches because their focus is not on the identification of the rights to be recognised based on human needs, but rather on the identification of the needs to be fulfilled and on the related obligations, even those 'imperfect obligations' that do not correspond to a right (2004: 204–5). The most well-known example of such an approach is represented by O'Neill's (2008) perspective that, based on Kant's thinking, defines human obligations as 'obligations never to act in ways which others cannot in principle also act' (2008: 150). Based on a system of principles of action derived from this main assumption, O'Neill then argues that persons in need, being vulnerable and not self-sufficient, are incapable 'to become and to remain autonomous agents who could act on principles that can be universally shared' (2008: 152). She goes on to argue that if we are committed to treat others as agents who can 'share the same principles as we do', we then have the obligation not to be indifferent to others' needs and to help them in sharing the same principle of action, that is to achieve and to maintain their autonomy. In this context, not only is the obligation of material aid justified, but it must also be based on the recognition and enhancement, through the

DOI: 10.1057/9781137505903.0006

creation of adequate socioeconomic and political arrangements, of poor and vulnerable people's skills, participation and active role in order to enable them to gain and maintain independence and control over their life (2008: 152–3). Acknowledging that no individual or institution can do everything, O'Neill concludes that 'no individual and no institution is prevented from making those decisions within its power in ways that help fulfil rather than spurn obligations to the hungry' (2008: 154–5). Recalling that these principles are part of Christian and other traditions as well as intrinsic to common social behaviour, O'Neill, as Trujillo points out, leaves room in her theory for a crucial role to be played by 'social and institutional virtues' (O'Neill quoted in Trujillo 2004: 205). In this sense, according to Trujillo, her theory would fall within the domain of (asymmetrical) *benevolence* and not within that of symmetrical and *reciprocal* justice (2004: 205–6).

Theories of distributive justice may also be based on cooperative schemes, such as in the case of contractualist theories. Amongst them, the most famous is Rawls's theory of justice that he extended to the international domain in his *The Law of Peoples* (1999). Although analysing Rawls's well-known justice theory falls outside the scope of this book (see Wenar 2001, Gozzi 2010: 231–44), it is to be highlighted that Rawls's theory includes a limited 'duty of assistance' by well-ordered peoples towards 'burdened societies', that is societies 'burdened by unfavourable conditions' (Rawls 1999: 106). However, Rawls does not intend such duty as a 'principle of distributive justice' because its aim is 'to realize and preserve just (or decent) institutions' in those societies, and not simply to increase their average level of wealth (1999: 107). Rawls' theory can be usefully analysed by briefly contrasting it with Beitz's and Pogge's cosmopolitan arguments for global redistributive justice, as the three scholars have also explicitly engaged in their respective writings in a debate on the matter.

Comparing the lack of substantial and effective initiatives against poverty by developed countries with their increased level of military intervention against human rights violations in developing ones, Pogge (2001) argues that the moral duty of developed countries to help in material terms derives from: their involvement in the production of world poverty through their contribution to the phenomena of genocide, colonialism and slavery; the benefits they obtain from natural resources by excluding, without compensation, poor countries; and the perpetuation and aggravation of global economic inequality through the shaping

DOI: 10.1057/9781137505903.0006

of an unequal global economic order, particularly by means of bribery and of the international borrowing and resource privileges (2001: 14–15, see 18–21 and 2008). Similarly, Beitz argues that a 'global difference principle' should apply based on the recognition of the fact that scarce natural resources, as well as technology and human capital and position in the international political economy, are unevenly distributed amongst countries and that, in the contemporary interdependent economic world, nations cannot be considered as self-sufficient as they are *unequal* in a global system within which conditions are designed by stronger members, and thus produce benefits for some members and unavoidable burdens for others (1975: 368–75, see also 2000: 688–94).[15]

On the contrary, Rawls assumes that the root causes for wealth accumulation of a people lie in 'the political culture, the political virtues and civic society of the country' that support its social and political institutions, as well as in the industriousness, probity and capacity for innovation of its members, and in the country's population policy (1999: 108–10). Based on this assumption, Rawls advocates for a *transitional* duty of assistance that has a target, and a cut-off point for it holds until all societies have achieved 'just liberal or decent institutions', that are the 'essentials of *political autonomy*' (1999: 118). In analogy with the domestic domain, Rawls in fact argues that his theory does not hold that equality is just or good in itself, but rather that 'inequalities are not always unjust' and when they are unjust it is 'because of their unjust effects' on the basic structure of the Society of Peoples (1999: 113–14).[16] In this sense, just as in domestic sphere the gap between rich and poor cannot be wider than the criterion of reciprocity permits and thus the aim is not to make all citizens equal in wealth, similarly, in the context of the Society of Peoples, once the objective of assistance is reached, and thus 'all peoples have a working liberal or decent government', there is no reason to further reduce the gap between rich and poor peoples (1999: 114).

The discussion of aid as a *moral* obligation sketched earlier intersects so many other different problematic domains that it is impossible to address all the various, complex implications that derive from those intersections.[17] The analysis of the logic of the foreign aid regime developed in the previous chapter and section reveals that the relationship with moral perspectives, principles and values is not something external to it but rather internal. It is internal by being intrinsic not only to its rhetoric and discourse but also to its operations as a '*moral activity*' (Dean 2010: 19, emphasis added). The foreign aid regime builds in fact upon

DOI: 10.1057/9781137505903.0006

shared and highly valuable moral concerns and intentions. It implies more or less explicit assumptions about what constitutes 'good, virtuous, appropriate, responsible conduct of individuals and collectives' (2010: 19). It is concerned with designing technologies and mechanisms that can maintain and enhance its credibility as a virtuous endeavour. But the moral dimension of aid also operates in a specific way in relation to the conceptualisation of the international domain. As Aaltola effectively highlights in relation in particular to food aid:

> the altruistic language of famine aid attains its political presence and becomes persuasive and alluring just because it refers to and contrasts with the negative side of international power politics. Thus, the perceived anarchic nature of international relations that renders international acts of altruism power-politically meaningful, persuasive and consequently useful, also fuels the worth of and gives 'soul' to the disinterested side of international relations. The act of gift-giving – international food aid – needs to be understood in its intricate and complex totality. The complexity results from the simultaneous existence of two distinct spheres of meaning creation, namely, that of international relations and that of conscientious humanitarian actions. Gift-giving can be a power-political phenomenon as long as international food aid remains a moral necessity on some other level. (Aaltola 1999: 385–6)

The thing with foreign aid is in fact that it allows donors to simultaneously address (their) international/global imperatives of *order* (security) and *justice*.

Conclusion: playing communitas against immunitas, and the other way round

> *Idem velle atque idem nolle,*
> *ea demum firma amicitia est.*
> (*Sallust, Conspiracy of Catiline, XX:4*)

Those which I have termed as cooperative/transformative and conflictual/conservative interpretations of gift-giving are useful also to address the peculiar ways in which the foreign aid regime constructs and puts into practice the idea of *interdependence* and of *international community*.

As illustrated by the literature on gift, gift-giving practices are ambiguously connected with the idea of community for there is no consensus

DOI: 10.1057/9781137505903.0006

on whether they are to be intended as the expression of an already existing community, or they themselves provide grounds for the creation of a community (Osteen 2002: 5). Comparing the operations of the gift with Hobbes's social contract theory, Verhezen has for instance highlighted that Maussian gift-giving practices construct 'decentralized' relationships against chaos and war in contrast with the centralised solution that is provided through the creation of the Leviathan (2005: 28–34). However, according to Hénaff's reinterpretation of the Maussian gift as *ceremonial gift-giving*, as a procedure of 'public and reciprocal recognition' (2010b: 69), such kind of gift-giving would be at the origin of the creation of a *community*.

Recalling the classical Greek and Roman procedure of the *pact* performed through a *symbolon* (from *ballein*: to put; and *syn*: together), Hénaff emphasises that the gift, as the symbolon, witnesses *for the future* the commitment that has been made between the giver and the receiver, the *alliance* that has been established (2010b: 71). In this sense, it would represent a decision to commit, a '*personal gesture* of commitment' which, in line with the rules of gift-giving, requires a counter-gift (2010b: 73). The obligation to return the gift, which is not a moral duty, nor a true legal obligation, makes it visible, according to Hénaff, that gift-giving is a *game*: as in a throw ball game, 'entering the game entails having to reply' because not to reply is tantamount to leaving the game (2010b: 74). Going further, Hénaff argues that 'as an institutional procedure between groups', ceremonial gift-giving constitutes 'the very emergence of a *public order* – though not necessarily its permanent historical form' (2010b: 75). With the emergence of a power entity, such as the polis or the state, public reciprocal recognition that was ensured by gift-giving practices in traditional societies is ensured by the law before which individuals are equal, and which pertains to the middle, in-between space between individuals. In this new scenario, dual, agonistic reciprocity is replaced by contractual mutuality (2010b: 75–8).

In this context, provided that the 'Golden Rule' of the game, that is *reciprocal recognition*, is respected, ceremonial gift-giving is intended as a preliminary step to control conflict and to provide grounds for the establishment of the political and legal institutions that ensures the life of a community of *equal* members (2010b: 79). Similarly to the process of communication, in which the exchange of words is the acceptance of a process of mediation that presupposes the world and at the same time makes it speakable, gift-giving can thus be considered

DOI: 10.1057/9781137505903.0006

as a mediation that brings *interdependence* into the relationship and makes it common/appropriable and shapeable in a non-conflictual way (see 2010b: 79).

The connection between the gift and the idea of community has also been investigated by Esposito in *Communitas* (2010). Analysing the complex etymology of the word community, Esposito highlights that the first meaning of *communitas*, and of its corresponding adjective *communis*, relates to something which is not *proper* and which 'begins when what is proper ends' (2010: 3). A second meaning can be gleaned from the word from which *communitas* itself is derived that is *munus*. Munus oscillates amongst three different meanings that are *onus*, *officium* and *donum* and that are all traceable to the idea of 'obligation'. Whereas the first two meanings are closely related to the idea of obligation, as they mean office, official, position and post, the general use of *donum* or gift does not seem to imply a relation with the idea of duty. However, as Esposito explains, *munus* denotes a particular gift, a gift that has an obligatory nature (2010: 4–5). It implies the idea of a 'tribute', of a 'pledge' that has to be paid, of an 'obligation' contracted with the other, of 'giving something that one can *not keep* [...] and over which, therefore, one is not completely master' (2010: 5).

In this sense, the *communitas* 'is the totality of persons united not by a "property" but precisely by an obligation or a debt' and *communis* is he 'who is required to carry out the functions of an office – or to the dona-tion [...] of a grace'; contrary, 'immune' is he who 'has to perform no office [...] and for that reason he remains *ungrateful*' (2010: 6, emphasis added). As Esposito further argues, 'Whereas the *communitas* is bound by the sacrifice of the *compensation* the *immunitas* implies the benefici-ary of the *dispensatio*' (2010: 6). More specifically, the 'immune' is the opposite of the 'common' in that it empties the common not only of 'its effects but also of its own presupposition'; it negates the 'very same foundations of community'; it introduces a violent separation between the two *inseparable* faces contained in the concept of *munus*, that is 'gift and obligation, benefit and service rendered, joining and threat'. Defining modernity as an 'immunitarian' project, Esposito highlights how modernity is construed as an order composed of isolated, separated individuals who are 'freed in advance from the "debt" that binds them one to the other'; 'exonerated', 'relieved' of the relation with the other that 'threatens' their identity and exposes them to risk of conflict and 'contagion' (2010: 12–13).

DOI: 10.1057/9781137505903.0006

The sole brief reference to these reflections, which does not reflect their richness and extension, and the attempt to translate them into the international domain, allows to highlight that, as already emphasised in other parts of the study, it is the dual, ambiguous nature of gift-giving practices that peculiarly nurtures from many points of view the operations of foreign aid regime and that gives rise to ambiguous elaborations of the idea of *interdependence* and of *international community*.

Political realism, for instance, highlights the conflictual/conservative potential of foreign aid and the role it carries as part of a domination strategy. It considers foreign aid as a foreign policy tool to preserve hierarchical power relations, security and order in an intrinsically anarchical international domain. Within this approach, there is little appreciation for the transformative/cooperative potential of foreign aid. It is this transformative/cooperative potential that carries with it not only the idea of the existence of an international community but also the promise of a *change*, of a more equal, free and just community. But this transformative/cooperative potential does not simply constitute, as realist thinkers argue, a rhetorical, ideological dimension (see Morgenthau 1962). Rather it is an integral component of the foreign aid regime governmental rationality. Foreign aid practices allow the *conservation* of order, hierarchy and inequality because they operate *through* the freedom, active engagement and responsibilisation of recipients; they operate *through* a *material and ethical promise* of *transformation*, of a new order, freedom and equality. It is their transformative/cooperative potential that allows foreign aid programmes, knowledge and various techniques to continue to operate. In addition, realist perspectives fail to adequately appreciate the fact that within the foreign aid regime the state is only one component, though a rather important one, of a complex assemblage of different governmental actors and entities.

Similarly, whereas liberal internationalism emphasises the cooperative/transformative dimension of foreign aid practices, that is their being part of the construction of a more equitable international community based upon cooperation, common rules and universal principles, it is not able to problematise the conservative/conflictual potential that foreign aid gift carries with it. It does not satisfactorily explain in which ways hierarchical relations are maintained and perpetuated through foreign aid gift. Or how international principles together with moral imperatives contribute to the *conservation of distance* between donors and recipients.

DOI: 10.1057/9781137505903.0006

Indeed, the operations of the foreign aid regime in a peculiar fashion contribute to construct the notion of interdependence. Within the foreign aid regime, interdependence is made governable and thinkable as a 'natural' and, at the same time, 'artificial' condition. It can be investigated, scrutinised and ordered and yet it remains intrinsically elusive, obscure and disordered. More crucially, the question of interdependence is still made governable through the *opposition* between sameness and difference. Order arises from sameness, disorder arises from difference.

Through foreign practices donors are constructed as the sole *communes* who are paying the common 'debt', working for the order of interdependence, and thus for the community. Recipients are reduced to being part of it only as the ungrateful *immune*, though a peculiar version of the *immune*. They are not freed from the debt, or exonerated by services and obligations towards the community. But they remain those who potentially negate the 'very same foundations of community', the cause of potential disorder. Thus, interdependence becomes the reason for the necessary, *selective* forms of 'immunisation' of donors against recipients. It is the reason behind the development of varied technologies of defence against the possible 'contagion'. Donors are the guarantors of the order; they are still the 'trustees' of the international community. Recipients are the cause of potential disorder; they are still the subjects under 'trusteeship'. In conclusion, it seems that the ultimate level at which the double bind logic intrinsic to the gift operates is represented by the continuous interplay between communitas and immunitas, between order and disorder. Communitas requires immunisation against the immune. Order requires intervention, disorder against the disordered.

Foreign aid gift does not work as a proper Maussian gift or as a solidarity-based gift for it is constructed as a peculiar form of *gracious gift*. It does not create a space of *reciprocal recognition*. It does not contribute to the re-building of interdependence as a new, *common* and *communicative* in-between space, as an *inter*-national space of dialogue between *different truths* (Owens 2007: 146–7). It does not create a new space where the Arendtian pluralistic *friendship* and *solidarity* may blossom. It opens and maintains a space where the binary logic of sameness and difference in various ways and at various levels operates. It opens and maintains a *conservative* space in which *transformation* is always *yet-to-come*.

DOI: 10.1057/9781137505903.0006

Notes

1 The field of development critique is a vast and rich domain whose detailed investigation is not within the scope of this study, even though many of its insights have informed it. Amongst the many, for a detailed analysis of the strengths and weaknesses of: dependency and world system theory, see Rist (2008), Conway and Heynen (2008), Kapoor (2008) and Klak (2008); post-structural theories, see Sidaway (2008) and Escobar (2012); postcolonial ones, see Kapoor (2008) and McEwan (2008).

2 This attempt to consider simultaneously the two perspectives is largely inspired by the interesting and very useful 'mutual critique' Kapoor stages between dependency and postcolonial theory by reading the one against the other, see Kapoor (2008: 3–18).

3 According to Simpson, the principle of sovereign equality encompasses three distinct forms of equality, namely 'formal equality', 'legislative equality' and 'existential equality'. While states' formal equality is commonly recognized in the international domain, their legislative and existential equality has been periodically compromised, as Simpson argues, by the presence of legalised hierarchies (legalised hegemony and anti-pluralism) that 'modify sovereign equality' and produce what he terms 'juridical sovereignty' (see 2004: ix–22, 37–56). For the definition of 'juridical sovereignty' and the role this concept plays in Simpson's analysis, see Simpson (2004: ix–37).

4 For an extensive conceptual and discursive analysis of Western international law, from its ancestors to its contemporary evolutions, and particularly of its connections with Western civilising mission, colonialism and neocolonialism, see Gozzi (2010).

5 Simpson uses the expression 'Great Powers' to indicate 'an elite group of states' that occupies 'a position of authority' within a legal regime. This authority derives from a position of 'assumed cultural, material and legal superiority' and entails the policing of the international order and 'a right to intervene in the affairs of other states in order to promote some proclaimed community goal' (2004: 5).

6 For a critical discussion of the right to self-determination and of the role peoples and movements should be attributed according to alternative visions and approaches to international law, such as those propounded by the TWAIL – Third World Approaches International Law network, see Gozzi (2010: 371–81).

7 For an interesting and recent analysis of the evolution of state sovereignty in relation to both the evolution of the concepts of human rights and of the rights of peoples, see Gozzi (2010).

DOI: 10.1057/9781137505903.0006

8   Both the notion of 'sovereignty as responsibility' and the 'responsibility to protect' principle confer a responsibility on states to ensure the well-being and protection of their citizens. They also confer a responsibility on the international community to assist/intervene when states fail to carry out their responsibilities. On the evolution from the first notion towards the second and on the 'responsibility to protect' principle, whose analysis falls outside the scope of this book, see, amongst the many, Deng (2010), Bellamy and Drummond (2011) and Philpott (2014).

9   In the case of failure of conservatorships, Helman and Ratner argue that 'It is even conceivable that a better solution might be a referendum by the citizens of the state on partition or union with a neighbor' (1992–3: 19).

10 A more recent example of this argument is represented by Pogge's theory, which is discussed further in this section. See also Satz (2005).

11 On development ethics, along with Crocker's writing, see also Qizilbash (1996), Gasper (2007) and Astroulakis (2013).

12 As to the relation between justice and benevolence, Trujillo (2004) emphasises that even though benevolence does not relate to compulsory duties, it is however true that not to help a person who is in need elicits condemnation with regard to the common 'sense of justice', and thus benevolence is to be deemed somehow related with justice. The actions of benevolence are commonly defined, following the Bible parable, as 'samaritan actions' that is the field around which revolve various theoretical reflections on the duty to help that go under the name of 'samaritanism' (2004: 187–9).

13 The elaboration of this part is mainly informed by Opeskin (1996) and Trujillo (2004).

14 Singer elaborates two different versions of his theory, the one described earlier and a 'weaker' version, which however he does not favour, according to which a person is obliged to prevent something bad from happening if they can do it 'without sacrificing anything morally significant' (2008: 3). To the two different versions correspond two different extensions of the duty to give (2008: 12–13). See also Opeskin (1996: 24–6).

15 Beitz's and Pogge's theories are obviously far richer in both their assumptions and proposals than what has been briefly outlined. For an interesting analysis of both theories in comparison with Rawls's one, see Wenar (2001).

16 Another sharp difference between Beitz's and Pogge's theories and Rawls's one is in fact that, as Rawls himself explains, 'the ultimate concern of a cosmopolitan view is the well-being of individuals', whereas the Law of Peoples is concerned with 'the justice of societies' (1999: 119).

17 On the limitations of human rights theories and discourse, see for instance Kapoor (2008: 33–8), Gozzi (2010: 266–73) and Silk (2004: 238–46). They

DOI: 10.1057/9781137505903.0006

argue that there is a need to contextualise human rights with reference to their *cultural* origin, dimension and construction in order to recognise their limitations and risks. They also propose that human rights are promoted within the context of cross-cultural learning, dialogue and practices.

DOI: 10.1057/9781137505903.0006

References

Aaltola, M. (1999) 'Emergency Food Aid as a Means of Political Persuasion in the North Korean Famine', *Third World Quarterly*, 20(2), 371–86.

Abuzeid, F. (2009) 'Foreign Aid and the "Big Push" Theory: Lessons from Sub-Saharan Africa', *Stanford Journal of International Relations*, XI(1), 16–23.

Alkire, S. (2002) 'Dimensions of Human Development', *World Development*, 30(2), 181–205.

Anders, G. (2005) 'Good Governance as Technology: Towards an Ethnography of the Bretton Woods Institutions' in D. Mosse and D. Lewis (eds) *The Aid Effect. Giving and Governing in International Development* (London; Ann Arbor, MI: Pluto Press).

Annan, K. (1998) *Thirty-Fifth Annual Ditchley Foundation Lecture*, 26 June 1998. http://www.un.org/press/en/1998/19980626.sgsm6613.html, date accessed 3 September 2014.

Arendt, H. (1968[1960]) *Men in Dark Times* (New York: Harcourt, Brace & World).

Arendt, H. (1990[1963]) (1990) *On Revolution* (London: Penguin Books).

Astroulakis, N. (2013) 'Ethics and International Development: The Development Ethics Paradigm', *East–West Journal of Economics and Business*, XVI(1), 99–117.

Athané, F. (2008), *Le don. Histoire du concept, évolution des pratiques* (Thèse de doctorat, Paris: Université Paris X).

Beitz, C.R. (1975) 'Justice and International Relations', *Philosophy and Public Affairs*, 4(4), 360–89.

DOI: 10.1057/9781137505903.0007

Beitz, C.R. (2000) 'Rawls's Law of Peoples', *Ethics*, 110(4), 669–96.

Beitz, C.R. (2001) 'Does Global Inequality Matter?', *Metaphilosophy*, 32(1/2), 95–112.

Bellamy, A.J. and C. Drummond (2011) 'The Responsibility to Protect in Southeast Asia: Between Non-Interference and Sovereignty as Responsibility', *The Pacific Review*, 24(2), 179–200.

Benson, M. and D. Carter (2008) 'Introduction: Nothing in Return? Distinctions between Gift and Commodity in Contemporary Societies', *Anthropology in Action*, 15(3), 1–7.

Benveniste, É. (1969) *Le vocabulaire des institutions indo-européennes. 2. Pouvoir, droit, religion* (Paris: Les Éditions de Minuit).

Binns, T. (2008) 'Dualistic and Unilinear Concepts of Development' in V. Desai and R.B. Potter (eds) *The Companion to Development Studies*, 2nd edn (London: Hodder Education).

Birch, T.D. (1998) 'An Analysis of Adam Smith's Theory of Charity and the Problems of the Poor', *Eastern Economic Journal*, 24(1), 25–41.

Black, M. (2004) *La cooperazione allo sviluppo internazionale* (Roma: Carocci) [originally in English *The No-Nonsense Guide to International Development*. Oxford: New Internationalist™ Publications, 2002].

Bourdieu, P. (1990) *The Logic of Practice* (Stanford, CA: Stanford University Press) [originally in French *Le sens pratique*. Paris: Les Éditions de Minuit, 1980].

Bourdieu, P. (1998) *Practical Reason. On the Theory of Action* (Stanford, CA: Stanford University Press) [originally in French *Raison Pratiques*. Paris: Éditions du Seuil, 1994].

Boutros-Ghali, B. (1992) *An Agenda for Peace. Preventive Diplomacy, Peacemaking and Peace-Keeping*, Report of the Secretary-General, 17 June 1992. http://www.cfr.org/peacekeeping/report-un-secretary-general-agenda-peace/p23439, date accessed 3 September 2014.

Brezzi, F. (2008) 'Philía e dono. Dall'identità singolare verso un nuovo legame sociale', *Bollettino della società filosofica italiana*, CXCV, 43–58.

Brezzi, F. (2011) 'Introduzione' in F. Brezzi and M.T. Russo (eds) *Oltre la società degli individui. Teoria ed etica del dono* (Torino: Bollati Boringhieri).

Brinkerhoff, D.W. (2008) 'The State and International Development Management: Shifting Tides, Changing Boundaries, and Future Directions', *Public Administration Review*, November/December, 985–1001.

DOI: 10.1057/9781137505903.0007

Carlà, F. and M. Gori (2014) 'Introduction' in F. Carla and M. Gori (eds) *Gift-Giving and the Embedded Economy in the Ancient World*, Akademiekonferenzen (Heidelberg: Universitätsverlag Winter).

Ceron, A. (2012) 'Sull'amicizia politica', *Storia del Pensiero Politico*, 1, 143–57.

Conway, D. and N. Heynen (2008) 'Dependency Theories: From ECLA to André Gunder Frank and Beyond' in V. Desai and R.B. Potter (eds) *The Companion to Development Studies*, 2nd edn (London: Hodder Education).

Cowen, M. and R.W. Shenton (1996) *Doctrines of Development* (London: Routledge).

Crocker, D.A. (2001) 'Globalization and Human Development: Ethical Approaches' in E. Malinvaud and L. Sabourin (eds), *Globalization. Ethical and Institutional Concerns* (Vatican City: Pontifical Academy of Social Science).

Cullather, N. (2000) 'Development? It's History', *Diplomatic History*, 24(4), 641–53.

Dardot, P. and C. Laval (2013) *The New Way of the World: On Neoliberal Society* (London; New York: Verso) [originally in French *La nouvelle raison du monde: Essai sur la société néolibérale*. Paris: La Découverte, 2009].

Davis, N. Zemon (2000) *The Gift in Sixteenth-Century France* (Madison: University of Wisconsin Press).

Davis, N. Zemon (2014) *The Gift – Bibliography*. http://science.jrank.org/pages/7732/Gift.html, date accessed 17 August 2014.

Dean, M. (2007) *Governing Societies: Political Perspectives on Domestic and International Rule*, Issues in Society (Maidenhead; New York: Open University Press).

Dean, M. (2010) *Governmentality. Power and Rule in Modern Society*, 2nd edn (London: Sage).

Deng, F.M. (2010). 'From "Sovereignty as Responsibility" to the "Responsibility to Protect"', *Global Responsibility to Protect*, 2(4), 353–70.

Derrida, J. (1992) *Given Time: I. Counterfeit Money* (Chicago; London: The University of Chicago Press) [originally in French *Donner le temps*. Paris: Éditions Galilée, 1991].

Douglas, M. (2002) 'Foreword' in M. Mauss *The Gift. The Form and Reason for Exchange in Archaic Societies* (London: Routledge) [originally in French *Essai sur le don*. Paris: Presses Universitaires de France, 1950].

DOI: 10.1057/9781137505903.0007

Dovolich, C. (2006) 'Per Jacques Derrida. Amicizia e Ospitalità', *Babelonline*, 2, 55–64 (http://www.babelonline.net).

Duffield, M. (2001a) 'Governing the Borderlands: Decoding the Power of Aid', *Disasters*, 25(4), 308–20.

Duffield, M. (2001b) *Global Governance and the New Wars. The Merging of Development and Security* (London; New York: Zed Books).

Duffield, M. (2002) 'Social Reconstruction and the Radicalization of Development: Aid as a Relation of Global Liberal Governance', *Development and Change*, 33(5), 1049–71.

Duffield, M. (2007) *Development, Security and Unending War. Governing the World of Peoples* (Cambridge: Polity Press).

Duffield, M. (2013) 'How Did We Become Unprepared? Emergency and Resilience in an Uncertain World', *British Academy Review*, 21, 55–8.

Eade, D. (ed.) (1998) *Development and Rights* (Oxford, UK: Oxfam Great Britain).

Easterly, W. (2005) 'Reliving the '50s: The Big Push, Poverty Traps, and Takeoffs in Economic Development', *Working Paper 65* (Center for Global Development: http://www.cgdev.org).

Eggen, Ø. and K. Roland (2014) *Western Aid at a Crossroads: The End of Paternalism*, Palgrave Pivot (Basingtoke: Palgrave Macmillan).

Escobar, A. (2012) *Encountering Development. The Making and Unmaking of the Third World. With a New Preface by the Author* (Princeton: Princeton University Press).

Esposito, R. (2006) 'Amicizia e Comunità', *Babelonline*, 2, 65–72 (http://www.babelonline.net).

Esposito, R. (2010) *Communitas. The Origin and Destiny of Community* (Stanford, CA: Stanford University Press) [originally in Italian *Communitas: Origine e destino della comunità*. Torino: Einaudi, 1998, 2006].

EU (European Parliament, Directorate-General for External Policies of The Union) (2014) *Financing for Development Post-2015: Improving The Contribution Of Private Finance*. http://eurodad.org/files/pdf/5346a6b10e9a4.pdf, date accessed 4 July 2014.

Eyben, R. (2005) 'Donors' Learning Difficulties: Results, Relationships and Responsibilities', *IDS Bulletin*, 36(3), 98–107.

Eyben, R. (2006) 'The Power of the Gift and the New Aid Modalities', *IDS Bulletin*, 37(6), 88–98.

Eyben, R. and R. Léon (2005) 'Whose Aid? The Case of the Bolivian Elections Projects' in D. Mosse and D. Lewis (eds) *The Aid Effect.*

DOI: 10.1057/9781137505903.0007

Giving and Governing in International Development (London; Ann Arbor, MI: Pluto Press).

Eyben, R. et al. (2007) 'Participatory Action Research into Donor– Recipient Relations: A Case Study', *Development in Practice*, 17(2), 167–78.

Ferguson, J. (1994) *The Anti-Politics Machine: 'Development', Depoliticization, and Bureaucratic Power in Lesotho* (Minneapolis: University of Minnesota Press).

Ferguson, J. and A. Gupta (2002) 'Spatializing States: Toward an Ethnography of Neoliberal Governmentality', *American Ethnologist*, 29(4), 981–1002.

Frey, M. and S. Kunkel (2011), 'Writing the History of Development: A Review of the Recent Literature', *Contemporary European History*, 20(2), 215–32.

Fukuda-Parr, S. (2003) 'The Human Development Paradigm: Operationalizing Sen's Ideas on Capabilities', *Feminist Economics*, 9(2–3), 301–17.

Gasper, D. (2007) 'Human Rights, Human Needs, Human Development, Human Security: Relationships between Four International "Human" Discourses', *Working Paper 20* (GARNET: http://www.garnet-eu.org).

Ghai, D. P. et al. (1980) *The Basic-Needs Approach to Development. Some Issues Regarding Concepts and Methodology* 3rd edn (Geneva: International Labour Office).

Godbout, J.T. (2006) 'Le don au-delà de la dette', *Revue du MAUSS*, 1(27), 91–104.

Godbout, J.T. and A. Caillé (1998) *The World of the Gift* (Montreal: McGill-Queen's University Press) [originally in French *L'Esprit du don*. Paris; Montréal: La Découverte; Les Éditions du Boréal, 1992].

Gould, J. (2005) 'Timing, Scale and Style: Capacity as Governmentality in Tanzania' in D. Mosse and D. Lewis (eds) *The Aid Effect. Giving and Governing in International Development* (London; Ann Arbor, MI: Pluto Press).

Gozzi, G. (2010) *Diritti e civiltà. Storia e filosofia del diritto internazionale* (Bologna: il Mulino).

Gray, P.A. (2011) 'Looking "The Gift" in the Mouth. Russia as Donor', *Anthropology Today* 27(2), 5–8.

DOI: 10.1057/9781137505903.0007

Guenther, L. (2006) *The Gift of The Other. Levinas and The Politics of Reproduction*, SUNY series in Gender Theory (Albany: State University of New York Press).

Hancock, G. (1989) *Lords of Poverty. The Power, Prestige and Corruption of the International Aid Business* (New York: The Atlantic Monthly Press).

Hardin, G. (2008) 'Lifeboat Ethics: The Case Against Helping the Poor' in T. W. Pogge and K. Horton (eds) *Global Ethics: Seminal Essays*, vol. II (St Paul, MN: Paragon House).

Hattori, T. (2001) 'Reconceptualizing Foreign Aid', *Review of International Political Economy*, 8(4), 633–60.

Hattori, T. (2003) 'The Moral Politics of Foreign Aid', *Review of International Studies*, 29, 229–47.

HDR (Human Development Report) (2003) *Millennium Development Goals: A Compact among Nations to End Human Poverty*, United Nations Development Programme (New York; Oxford: Oxford University Press).

Helman, G.B. and S.R. Ratner (1992–3) 'Saving Failed States', *Foreign Policy*, 89, 3–20.

Hénaff, M. (2010a) *The Price of Truth. Gift, Money and Philosophy*. (Stanford: Stanford University Press) [originally in French *Le prix de la vérité*. Paris: Éditions du Seuil, 2002].

Hénaff, M. (2010b) 'I/You: Reciprocity, Gift-Giving, and the Third Party', *META: Res. in Herm. Phen. and Pract. Philosophy*, II (1), 57–83.

Hénaff, M. (2010c) 'On The Norm of Reciprocity', *Quaderno 2010* (Centro Studi Teoria e Critica della Regolazione Sociale: http://www.lex.unict.it/tcrs/).

Hjertholm, P. and H. White (2000) 'Survey of Foreign Aid: History, Trends and Allocation', *Discussion Papers 04* (Department of Economics, University of Copenhagen: http://www.econ.ku.dk/english/).

Hobbes, T. (1839[1651]) 'Leviathan, or the Matter, Form, and Power of a Commonwealth Ecclesiastical and Civil' in Sir W.B. Molesworth (ed.) *The English Works of Thomas Hobbes of Malmesbury*, vol. III (London: Bohn).

Hynes, W. and S. Scott (2013) 'The Evolution of Official Development Assistance: Achievements, Criticisms and a Way Forward', *OECD Development Co-operation Working Papers 12*, OECD Publishing.

Ivarsson Holgersson, C. (2013) *The Give and Take of Disaster Aid. Social and Moral Transformation in the Wake of the Tsunami in Sri Lanka*

DOI: 10.1057/9781137505903.0007

(Doctoral Dissertation in Social Anthropology, University of Gothenburg).

Jackson, R.H. (1990) *Quasi-States: Sovereignty, International Relations and the Third World*, Cambridge Studies in International Relations (Cambridge: Cambridge University Press).

Kapoor, I. (2008) *The Postcolonial Politics of Development* (London, New York: Routledge).

Kaul, I. et al. (eds) (1999) *Global Public Goods. International Cooperation in the 21st Century* (New York: Oxford University Press).

Keijzer, N. (2012) 'The Future of Development Cooperation: From Aid to Policy Coherence for Development?', *Paper April 2012* (European Centre for Development Policy Management: http://ecdpm.org/resources/).

Kindornay, S. and F. Reilly-King (2013) 'Promotion and Partnership: Bilateral Donor Approaches to the Private Sector' in ÖFSE – Österreichische Forschungsstiftung für Internationale Entwicklung (Hrsg.) *Private Sector Development. Ein neuer Businessplan für Entwicklung?*, Österreichische Entwicklungspolitik 2013 (Wien: Südwind Verlag).

Klak, T. (2008) 'World-Systems Theory: Cores, Peripheries and Semi-Peripheries' in V. Desai and R.B. Potter (eds) *The Companion to Development Studies*, 2nd edn (London: Hodder Education).

Knack, S. (2004) 'Does Foreign Aid Promote Democracy?', *International Studies Quarterly*, 48, 251–66.

Konstan, D. (2008) 'Aristotle on Love and Friendship', ΣΧΟΛΗ, 2, 207–12.

Kothari, U. (2005) 'From Colonial Administration to Development Studies: A Post-Colonial Critique of the History of Development Studies' in U. Kothari (ed.) *A Radical History of Development Studies. Individuals, Institutions and Ideologies* (London: Zed Books).

Kowalski, R. (2011) 'The Gift – Marcel Mauss and International Aid', *Journal of Comparative Social Welfare*, 27(3), 189–205.

Kuziemko, I and E. Werker (2006) 'How Much Is a Seat on the Security Council Worth? Foreign Aid and Bribery at the United Nations', *Journal of Political Economy*, 114(5), 905–30.

Laidlaw, J. (2002) 'A Free Gift Makes no Friends' in M. Osteen (ed.) *The Question of the Gift. Essays across Disciplines*, Routledge Studies in Anthropology (London: Routledge).

Lancaster, C. (2007) *Foreign Aid. Diplomacy, Development, Domestic Politics* (London, USA: The University of Chicago Press).

DOI: 10.1057/9781137505903.0007

Larzillière, P. (2012) 'Production of Norms and Securitization in Development Policies: From Human Security to Security Sector Reform', *Working Paper 13* (Issam Fares Institute: http://www.aub.edu. lb/ifi/Pages/ifi_wps.aspx).

Latouche, S. (2005) *L'occidentalisation du monde. Essai sur la signification, la portée et les limites de l' uniformisation planétaire. Préface inédite de l'auteur*, 3rd edn (Paris: La Découverte).

League of Nations (1919), *Covenant of the League of Nations*, 28 April 1919. http://www.refworld.org/docid/3dd8b9854.html, date accessed 18 September 2014.

Lemke, T. (2007) 'An Indigestible Meal? Foucault, Governmentality and State Theory', *Distinktion: Scandinavian Journal of Social Theory*, 8(2), 43–64.

Lie, J.H.S. (2005) *Developmentality: CDF and PRSP as Governance Mechanisms*. https://www.academia.edu/2243939/Developmentality._ CDF_and_PRSP_as_Governance_Mechanisms, date accessed 1 November 2014.

Liebersohn, H. (2011) *The Return of the Gift. European History of a Global Idea* (New York: Cambridge University Press).

Ludden, D. (2005) 'Development Regimes in South Asia: History and the Governance Conundrum' *Working Paper 5* (Department of Economics and Social Sciences, BRAC University: http://dspace. bracu.ac.bd/handle/10361/345).

Macrae, J. et al. (2004) *Aid to 'Poorly Performing' Countries: A Critical Review of Debates and Issues*, July 20004 (ODI – Overseas Development Institute: http://www.odi.org).

Magnani, E. (dir.) (2007) *Don et sciences sociales. Théories et pratiques croisées* (Dijon: EUD).

Mallard, G. (2010) '*The Gift* Revisited: Marcel Mauss on War, Debt and the Politics of Nations', *Working Paper 10-004* (Buffett Center for International and Comparative Studies: http://www.bcics. northwestern.edu).

Marramao, G. (2011) 'Lo scandalo del dono' in F. Brezzi and M.T. Russo (eds) *Oltre la società degli individui. Teoria ed etica del dono* (Torino: Bollati Boringhieri).

Marshall, A. et al. (2001) 'Policies to Roll-Back the State and Privatize? Poverty Reduction Strategy Papers Investigated', *Discussion Paper 120* (World Institute for Development Economics, UNU-WIDER: http:// www.wider.unu.edu).

DOI: 10.1057/9781137505903.0007

Maul, D. (2009) ' "Help Them Move the ILO Way": The International Labor Organization and the Modernization Discourse in the Era of Decolonization and the Cold War', *Diplomatic History*, 33(3), 387–404.

Mauss, M. (2002[1923–4]) *The Gift. The Form and Reason for Exchange in Archaic Societies* (London: Routledge) [originally in French *Essai sur le don*. Paris: Presses Universitaires de France, 1950].

Mawdsley, E. (2012) 'The Changing Geographies of Foreign Aid and Development Cooperation: Contributions from Gift Theory', *Transactions of the Institute of British Geographers*, 37, 256–72.

Mawulo-Yevugah, L. (2011) *Developmentality. Elites Consensus and Rhetoric on Multilateral Aid Reform in Africa* (Saarbrücken: LAP LAMBERT Academic Publishing).

McEwan, C. (2008) 'Post-Colonialism' in V. Desai and R.B. Potter (eds) *The Companion to Development Studies*, 2nd edn (London: Hodder Education).

McVety, A.K. (2008) 'Pursuing Progress: Point Four in Ethiopia', *Diplomatic History*, 32(3), 371–403.

Miller, P. and N. Rose (1990) 'Governing Economic Life', *Economy and Society*, 19(1), 1–31.

Min, E. K. (2002) 'Adam Smith and the Debt of Gratitude' in M. Osteen (ed.) *The Question of the Gift. Essays across Disciplines*, Routledge Studies in Anthropology (London: Routledge).

Moore, G. (2011) *Politics of the Gift. Exchanges in Poststructuralism* (Edinburgh: Edinburgh University Press).

Morgenthau, H. (1962) 'A Political Theory of Foreign Aid', *The American Political Science Review*, 56(2), 301–9.

Moss, T. et al. (2006) 'An Aid–Institutions Paradox? A Review Essay on Aid Dependency and State Building in Sub-Saharan Africa', *Working Paper 74* (Center for Global Development: http://www.cgdev.org).

Mosse, D. (2005a) 'Global Governance and the Ethnography of International Aid' in D. Mosse and D. Lewis (eds) *The Aid Effect. Giving and Governing in International Development* (London; Ann Arbor, MI: Pluto Press).

Mosse, D. (2005b) *Cultivating Development. An Ethnography of Aid Policy and Practice* (London; Ann Arbor, MI: Pluto Press).

Moyo, D. (2009) *Dead Aid: Why Aid Is not Working and How There Is Another Way for Africa* (New York: Farrar, Straus and Giroux).

Natali, C. (2008) 'L'amicizia secondo Aristotele', *Bollettino della società filosofica italiana*, CXCV, 13–27.

National Research Council et al. (1978) *The U.S. Government Foreign Disaster Assistance Program* (Washington, DC: National Academy of Science).

National Security Council Staff (1951) 'Proposed Transfer of the Point IV Program from the Department of State to the Economic Cooperation Administration' in F. Aandahl (ed.) *Foreign Relations of the United States, 1951. National Security Affairs; Foreign Economic Policy*, vol. 1 (Washington: Government Printing Office). http://digital.library.wisc.edu/1711.dl/FRUS.FRUS1951v01, date accessed 14 July 2014.

Naz, F. (2006) 'Arturo Escobar and the Development Discourse: an Overview', *Asian Affairs*, 28(3), 64–84.

Nederveen Pieterse, J. (2002) 'Global Inequality: Bringing Politics Back In', *Third World Quarterly*, 23(6), 1023–46.

Nepi, P. (2006) 'Amicizia e giustizia tra antico e moderno', *Babelonline*, 2, 181–91 (http://www.babelonline.net).

Nussbaum, M.C. (2000) 'Duties of Justice, Duties of Material Aid. Cicero's Problematic Legacy', *Journal of Political Philosophy*, 8(2), 176–206.

Nussbaum, M.C. and A.K. Sen (eds) (1993) *The Quality of Life* (Oxford: Clarendon Press).

Nyerere, J. (1967) *The Arusha Declaration*, 5 February 1967. https://www.marxists.org/subject/africa/nyerere/1967/arusha-declaration.htm, date accessed 7 August 2014.

O'Neill, O. (2008) 'Rights, Obligations and World Hunger' in T. W. Pogge and K. Horton (eds) *Global Ethics: Seminal Essays*, vol. II (St Paul, MN: Paragon House).

OECD (2008) 'Is It Oda?' Factsheet, November. http://www.oecd.org/investment/stats/34086975.pdf, date accessed 1 July 2014.

Offer, A. (1997) 'Between the Gift and the Market: The Economy of Regard', *Economic History Review*, L(3), 450–76.

Opeskin, B.R. (1996) 'The Moral Foundations of Foreign Aid', *World Development*, 24(1), 21–44.

Osteen, M. (2002) 'Introduction: Questions of the Gift' in M. Osteen (ed.) *The Question of the Gift. Essays across Disciplines*, Routledge Studies in Anthropology (London: Routledge).

Owens, P. (2007) *Between War and Politics. International Relations and the Thought of Hannah Arendt* (Oxford: Oxford University Press).

Passerin d'Entrèves, M. (1995) 'La cittadinanza nella filosofia politica di Hannah Arendt', *Working Paper 102* (ICPS Universitat Autònoma de

DOI: 10.1057/9781137505903.0007

Barcelona: http://www.icps.cat/archivos/WorkingPapers/WP_I_102. pdf).

Pearson, L.B. (1970) 'A New Strategy for Global Development', *The UNESCO Courier*, February, 4–14.

Pearson, L.B. (and Commission on International Development) (1969) *Partners in Development* (London: Pall Mall Press).

Philpott, D. (2014) 'Sovereignty', *The Stanford Encyclopedia of Philosophy* (Summer 2014 Edition), Edward N. Zalta (ed.). http://plato.stanford. edu/archives/sum2014/entries/sovereignty/>, date accessed 28 January 2015.

Pogge, T. W. (2001) 'Priorities of Global Justice', *Metaphilosophy*, 32(1/2), 6–24.

Pogge, T. W. (2008) *World Poverty and Human Rights. Cosmopolitan Responsibilities and Reforms*, 2nd edn (Cambridge, UK: Polity Press).

Potter, D.W. (2004) 'State Responsibility, Sovereignty, and Failed States'. https://www.adelaide.edu.au/apsa/docs_papers/Others/potter.pdf, date accessed 3 October 2014.

Potter, R.B. (2008) 'Theories, Strategies and Ideologies of Development' in V. Desai and R.B. Potter (eds) *The Companion to Development Studies*, 2nd edn (London: Hodder Education).

Procacci, G. (1998) *Governare la povertà. La società liberale e la nascita della questione sociale* (Bologna: il Mulino).

Qizilbash, M. (1996) 'Ethical Development', *World Development*, 24(7), 1209–21.

Raphael, D.D. and A.L. Macfie (1982) (eds) 'Introduction' in A. Smith (1982[1759]) *The Theory of Moral Sentiments* (Indianapolis: Liberty Fund).

Rapley, J. (2002) *Understanding Development. Theory and Practice in the Third World*, 2nd edn (London; Boulder: Lynne Rienner).

Rawls, J. (1999) *The Law of Peoples, with 'The Idea of Public Reason Revisited'* (Cambridge, MA: Harvard University Press).

Riddell, R.C. (2007) *Does Foreign Aid Really Work?* (Oxford: Oxford University Press).

Risdale, F. (2011) 'A Discussion of the Potlatch and Social Structure', *Totem: The University of Western Ontario Journal of Anthropology*, 3(2), Article 3. http://ir.lib.uwo.ca/totem/vol3/iss2/3, date accessed 5 July 2014.

Rist, G. (2008) *The History of Development: From Western Origins to Global Faith*, 3rd edn (London: Zed Books).

DOI: 10.1057/9781137505903.0007

Robinson, W. I (2002) 'Remapping Development in Light of Globalisation: From a Territorial to a Social Cartography', *Third World Quarterly*, 23(6), 1047–71.

Rocha Menocal, A. (2013) 'It's a Risky Business. Aid and New Approaches to Political Risk Management', July 2013 (ODI – Overseas Development Institute: http://www.odi.org).

Roodman, D. (2007) 'The Anarchy of Numbers: Aid, Development, and Cross-Country Empirics', *Working Paper 32* (Center for Global Development: http://www.cgdev.org).

Sahlins, M. (1968) 'Philosophie politique de l' "Essai sur le don"', *L'Homme*, 8(4), 5–17.

Sahlins, M. (1972) *Stone Age Economics* (Chicago and New York: Aldine-Atherton).

Satlow, M.L. (2013) 'Introduction' in M.L. Satlow (ed.) *The Gift in Antiquity*, The Ancient World: Comparative Histories (Malden, MA; Oxford; Chirchester: Wiley-Blackwell).

Satz, D. (2005) 'What Do We Owe the Global Poor? Response to *World Poverty and Human Rights*', *Ethics & International Affairs*, 19(1), 47–54.

Sen, A.K. (1999) *Development as Freedom* (New York: Oxford University Press).

Seneca, L.A. (2011) *On Benefits*, transl. by M. Griffin and B. Inwood (Chicago; London: The University of Chicago Press).

Severino, J.-M. and O. Ray (2009) 'The End of ODA: Death and Rebirth of a Global Public Policy', *Working Paper 167* (Center for Global Development: http://www.cgdev.org).

Shleifer, A. (2009) 'Peter Bauer and the Failure of Foreign Aid', *Cato Journal*, 29(3), 379–90.

Sidaway, J.D. (2008) 'Post-Development' in V. Desai and R.B. Potter (eds) .*The Companion to Development Studies*, 2nd edn (London: Hodder Education).

Silk, J. (2004) 'Caring at a Distance: Gift Theory, Aid Chains and Social Movements', *Social and Cultural Geography*, 5, 229–51.

Silva, K.C. da (2008) 'AID as Gift: An Initial Approach', *Mana*, 14(1), 141–60.

Simpson, G. (2004) *Great Powers and Outlaw States. Unequal Sovereigns in the International Legal Order* (Cambridge: Cambridge University Press).

Singer, P. (2008) 'Famine, Affluence, and Morality' in T. W. Pogge and K. Horton (eds) *Global Ethics: Seminal Essays*, vol. II (St Paul, MN: Paragon House).

DOI: 10.1057/9781137505903.0007

Skøtt Thomsen, S. (2007) *Responding to PEPFAR – How NGOs Navigate Aid Conditionalities* (Master's Thesis, Roskilde: University of Roskilde).

Slim, H. (1995) 'What Is Development?', *Development in Practice*, 5(2), 143–48.

Slim, H. (2002) "A Response to Peter Uvin – Making Moral Low Ground: Rights as the Struggle for Justice and the Abolition of Development', *PRAXIS. The Fletcher Journal of Development Studies*, XVII – 2002.

Smith, A. (2007[1776]) *An Inquiry in to the Nature and Causes of The Wealth of Nations* (Petersfield: Harriman House).

Soesastro, H. (2004) *Sustaining East Asia's Economic Dynamism: The Role of Aid.* http://www.oecd.org/pcd/31970823.pdf, date accessed 1 September 2014.

Stokke, O. (2009) *The UN and Development: From Aid to Cooperation*, United Nations Intellectual History Project Series (Bloomington: Indiana University Press).

Stokke, O. (ed.) (1989) *Western Middle Powers and Global Poverty. The Determinants of the Aid Policies of Canada, Denmark, the Netherlands, Norway and Sweden*, Norwegian Foreign Policy Studies no. 64 (Uppsala: The Scandinavian Institute of African Studies).

Strathern, M. (2000) 'The Tyranny of Transparency', *British Educational Research Journal*, 26(3), 309–21.

Tomasevski, K. (1993) *Development Aid and Human Rights Revisited* (London: Pinter Publishers).

Trujillo, I. (2004) 'Paradigmi della giustizia internazionale. Argomenti pro e contro il dovere di aiuto ai popoli svantaggiati', *Ragion pratica*, 22(1), 179–224.

Truman, H.S. (1949a) *Inaugural Address*, 20 January 1949. http://www.bartleby.com/124/pres53.html, accessed 14 July 2014.

Truman, H.S. (1949b) *Special Message to the Congress Recommending Point 4 Legislation*, 24 June 1949. http://www.trumanlibrary.org/publicpapers/index.php?pid=1156&st=139&st1=, date accessed 15 July 2014.

Truman, H.S. (1951) *Letters Relating to the International Development Advisory Board's Report on Foreign Economic Policy*, 11 March 1951. http://www.trumanlibrary.org/publicpapers/index.php?pid=262&st=53&st1=, date accessed 14 July 2014.

Tschirhart, C. (2011) 'Theory Talk #41: Mark Duffield on Human (In)security, Liberal Interventionism and Fortified Aid Compounds',

Theory Talks. http://www.theorytalks. org/2011/07/theory-talk-41. html, date accessed 21 July 2014.

UN (1945) *Charter of the United Nations*, 26 June 1945. http://www. un.org/en/documents/charter/, date accessed 1 July 2014.

UN (1948a) *Resolution no. 198 (III) Economic Development of Underdeveloped Countries*, Adopted by the General Assembly, 4 December 1948. http://www.un.org/documents/ga/res/3/ares3.htm, date accessed 1 July 2014.

UN (1948b) *Resolution no. 200 (III) Technical Assistance for Economic Development*, Adopted by the General Assembly, 4 December 1948. http://www.un.org/documents/ga/res/3/ares3.htm, date accessed 1 July 2014.

UN (1974) *Declaration on the Establishment of a New International Economic Order*, Resolution no. 3201(S-VI) adopted by the General Assembly, 1 May 1974. http://www.un-documents.net/s6r3201.htm, date accessed 1 July 2014.

UNDP (United Nations Development Programme – Bureau for Development Policy Democratic Governance) (2012) *Institutional and Context Analysis. Guidance Note*. http://www.undp.org/content/undp/en/home/librarypage/democratic-governance/oslo_governance_centre/Institutional_and_Context_Analysis_Guidance_Note/, date accessed 1 September 2014.

Unger, C.R. (2010) 'Histories of Development and Modernization: Findings, Reflections, Future Research', *H-Soz-u-Kult*, 9 December. http://hsozkult.geschichte.hu-berlin.de/forum/2010-12-001, date accessed 15 January 2014.

Van Gastel, J. and M. Nuijten (2005) 'The Genealogy of the "Good Governance" and "Ownership" Agenda at the Dutch Ministry of Development Cooperation' in D. Mosse and D. Lewis (eds) *The Aid Effect. Giving and Governing in International Development* (London; Ann Arbor, MI: Pluto Press).

Veca, S. (1981) 'Prefazione' in R.L. Meek, *Il cattivo selvaggio* (Milano: il Saggiatore).

Veen, A.M. van der (2011) *Ideas, Interests and Foreign Aid* (Cambridge: Cambridge University Press).

Verhezen, P. (2005) *Gifts and Bribes: An Essay on the Limits of Reciprocity* (PhD thesis, Leuven: Katholieke Universiteit).

Watt, P. (2005) 'Partnership in Policy-Based Lending' in The World Bank, *Conditionality Revisited. Concepts, Experiences, and Lessons*

DOI: 10.1057/9781137505903.0007

(Washington, DC: The International Bank for Reconstruction and Development/The World Bank).

WDR (World Development Report) (2014) *Risk and Opportunity. Managing Risk for Development* (Washington, DC: International Bank for Reconstruction and Development /The World Bank).

Weber, M. (1946[1920]) 'Religious Rejections of the World and Their Directions' in H.H. Gerth and C. Wright Mills (eds) *From Max Weber: Essays in Sociology* (New York: Oxford University Press).

Wenar, L. (2001) 'Contractualism and Global Economic Justice', *Metaphilosophy*, 32(1/2), 79–94.

Wight, M. (1987) 'An Anatomy of International Thought', *Review of International Studies*, 13(3), 221–7.

Williams, D. (2000) 'Aid and Sovereignty: Quasi-States and the International Financial Institutions', *Review of International Studies*, 26, 557–73.

Woodruff, M.K. (2002) 'The Ethics of Generosity and Friendship: Aristotle's Gift to Nietzsche?' in M. Osteen (ed.) *The Question of the Gift. Essays across Disciplines*, Routledge Studies in Anthropology (London: Routledge).

Zamagni, S. and L. Bruni (eds) (2013) *Handbook on the Economics of Reciprocity and Social Enterprise* (Cheltenhaum, UK; Northampton, MA: Edward Elgar).

Zanasi, M. (2007) 'Exporting Development: The League of Nations and Republican China', *Comparative Studies in Society and History*, 49(1), 143–69.

Zionkowski, L. and C. Klekar (eds) (2009) *The Culture of the Gift in Eighteenth-Century England* (New York: Palgrave Macmillan).

Index

Aaltola, Mika, 31, 87, 108
Abuzeid, Farah, 49
accountability
  and deniability, 67
  of donors, construction of,
    68
  gap, 66
  as a measurable domain,
    55, 70
  and ownership/
    participation, 53–4
  of recipients, construction
    of, 67–8
  upward, 66–7
  see also credibility; trust
Alkire, Sabina, 80n
Anders, Gerhard, 32, 52–4, 68,
  79n
Annan, Kofi, 95
Arendt, Hannah, 112
  on friendship and fraternity,
    98–100
Aristotle, 35n, 98
  on friendship, 27–8
Arusha Declaration, the, 74–5
Astroulakis, Nikos, 114n
Athané, François, 11, 12, 16, 35n

Bauer, Peter, 66
Bedjaoui, Mohammed, 101
'Beijing model' of foreign aid,
  64, 81n
Beitz, Charles R., 106, 107, 114n
Bellamy, Alex J., 114n

Benveniste, Émile, 35n
Binns, Tony, 49, 51
biopolitics, 62
Birch, Thomas D., 14, 15
Black, Maggie, 64, 66, 81n
Bodin, Jean, 89
Bourdieu, Pierre, 35n
  on gift-exchange, 23–4, 38,
    84
Boutros-Ghali, Boutros, 95
Brezzi, Francesca, 16
Brinkerhoff, Derick W., 80n
Bruni, Luigino, 10

Caillé, Alain, 16, 29, 35n
capacity-building, technology
  of, 55, 68
  and 'real' empowerment, 69
Carlà, Filippo, 10, 12, 35n
Ceron, Annalisa, 28
Charter of the United Nations,
  the, 45, 64, 90–1, 95, 100
China International Famine
  Relief Commission, 39
Cicero, Marcus Tullius, 103
community
  as communitas, 110
  and gift-giving: Esposito on,
    110; Hénaff on, 109–10;
    Seneca on, 25
  and immunitas, 110
  international, construction
    of, 45–7, 87–97, 101, 111–12
  see also interdependence

DOI: 10.1057/9781137505903.0008

conditionality, 68, 77
    embryonic form of, 52
    'hard', 52–3, 79n
    'soft', 54–5, 79n
    and sovereignty, 96
    technology of, 53–5
    see also good governance; ownership;
        participation
Conway, Dennis, 113n
Cowen, Michael, 62, 68, 87
credibility
    construction of, 67, 108
    as a source of power, 64–5
    see also under individual actors
Crocker, David A., 103, 114n
Cullather, Nick, 49

Dardot, Pierre, 10
Davis, Natalie Zemon, 11, 12, 35n
Dean, Mitchell, 5, 6, 8, 32–4, 36n, 38,
    42, 55, 60, 61, 73, 80n, 95, 107
De beneficiis, 25
debt, role/construction of
    Bourdieu on, 23
    in the foreign aid regimee 3–4, 76–8,
    112
    in gift-giving, 3, 19, 27, 67
Declaration on the Establishment of a
    New International Economic Order,
    the, see NIEO Declaration
Declaration on the Granting of
    Independence to Colonial Countries
    and Peoples, the, 91
Deng, Francis M., 114n
Derrida, Jacques, 28
    on the gift, 21–2
development
    as debt, 3–4, 76–8
    dependency critiques of, 50, 86–7,
    113n
    and foreign aid, 2, 26–7, 49
    history of (the concept of), 47–62
    human, 56, 58
    modernisation theories of, 41,
        48–50, 57
    postcolonial critique of, 86, 113n

post-structural critique of, 86–7, 113n
    right to, 100–1
    and sovereignty (Jackson on), 92–3
    sustainable, 56
    as a system of truth, knowledge and
        discourse, 2, 5, 38, 47–62
    as trusteeship, see trusteeship,
        development as
    and underdevelopment, 45–6, 48–9,
        54, 76, 85
    world system critique of, 50, 86, 113n
    see also developmentality
developmentality, 36n
development compacts, 101
donor states
    'historical catharsis' of, 46, 87
    as 'generous nations', construction
        of, 46–7, 76, 87
    relations amongst, 63–4, 69
    relations with non-DAC donors, 73
Douglas, Mary, 15
Dovolich, Claudia, 99
Drummond, Catherine, 114n
Duby, George, 35n
Duffield, Mark, 6, 32, 59–62, 80n, 83

Eade, Deborah, 80n
Easterly, William, 49
Eggen, Øyvind, 50, 52, 53, 56, 57, 60,
    64, 70, 79n, 81n
equality/inequality
    construction of, 76, 84–7, 97
    and poverty, see poverty, and
        inequality of states
Escobar, Arturo, 32, 113n
Esposito, Roberto, 85, 99, 110
Esteva, Gustavo, 47
European Union, the, 56, 63, 80n
Eyben, Rosalind, 31, 66–9, 101

Ferguson, James, 32, 65
foreign aid
    as bribery, 29–30, 80n
    as a contractual relationship, 68
    definition of, see ODA
    as entitlement/obligation, 101–3

foreign aid – *Continued*
as a form of gift, 3, 5, 31–2, 75–8, 87, 100
as a moral obligation, *see* moral duty of material aid
foreign aid practices
and accountability/sovereignty of recipient states, 66–7, 83, 95–6
and corruption, 66
'double bind' logic of, 75–6, 111
historical origins of, 39–43
internationalization of, *see* League of Nations
interpretation of: 'conflictual', 83, 85–6, 97; 'cooperative', 84, 92–3, 97–8; by liberal internationalism, 4, 100–1, 111; by political realism, 4, 100, 111
as moral practices, 2–4, 50, 73, 107–8
as a regime of practices, *see* foreign aid regime
as technical and measurable practices, 2, 7, 41–2, 44–6, 49, 54, 58, 62, 70, 72, 83
as unreciprocated gift-giving practices, 3, 76–7, 112
foreign aid regime, the, 47–79
emergence of, 43–7
governmental strategies of, 48–69, 70, 72, 78
intrinsic logic of, 70–8
as a regime of practices of government, 2, 5, 6
relations with other regimes of international government, 79, 94
'technologies of agency' of, 55–6, 61, 80n
'technologies of performance' of, 53–5, 80n
Foucault, Michel, 3, 32, 33, 36n, 38, 69
Frey, Marc, 39, 63
Fukuda-Parr, Sakiko, 80n

Gasper, Des, 80n, 114n
General Assembly resolution 198 (III), 42–3

General Assembly resolution 200 (III), 42–3
Ghai, Dharam P., 51
gift, the concept of
and bribery, 16, 29, 36n
commonsense use of, 21
as conveying a pluriverse, 28–9
as defined *per differentiam*, 16
'double bind' of, 5, 22, 112
as an excessive concept, 29
history of, 11–17
'positioning' of, 11–12
see also Hénaff, and categories of gift-giving
Gift, The, 17–21, 35n
Mallard's interpretation of, 30–1
gift-giving
in antiquity, 11–12, 24–8
and the building of trust, 20–1, 26, 67
in the international domain, 29–31
in the 'modernised' age, 12–17
and recognition, 19, 24, 78, 83–4, 87, 97, 109
and time lapse: Mauss on, 19–20; Bourdieu on, 23
see also community, and gift-giving
Godbout, Jacques T., 16, 29
good governance, technology of, 3, 52–4
Gori, Maja, 10, 12, 35n
Gould, Jeremy, 32, 53–5, 64, 65, 68, 69, 75
government
analytics of, 5, 6, 8, 32–5
definition of, 32
and governance, 36n
regime of practices of, definition of, 33–4
and self-government, 3–4, 33, 55, 111
governmentality, 3, 32, 36n
see also developmentality
Gozzi, Gustavo, 81n, 106, 113n, 114n
Gray, Patty A., 31, 73, 81n
Greek-Turkish Aid Act, the, 42
Guenther, Lisa, 10
Gupta, Akhil, 32, 65

DOI: 10.1057/9781137505903.0008

Hancock, Graham, 66, 103
Hardin, Garrett, 104
Hattori, Tomohisa, 3, 6, 31, 73, 76, 100
Helman, Gerald B., 96, 97, 114n
Hénaff, Marcel, 30, 35n
    and categories of gift-giving:
    ceremonial gift-giving, 24;
    gracious gift-giving, 24–6;
    solidarity-based gift-giving, 26–8,
    84
Heynen, Nikolas, 113n
Hjertholm, Peter, 39
Hobbes, Thomas, 30, 109
    on gift-giving, 12–14
human capabilities, 56, 103
human rights, 5, 54, 55, 56, 80n, 81n, 85,
    93, 94, 95, 96, 101, 105, 106, 113n,
    114n, 115n
human rights-based approach to
    development, 65, 103
human security, 5, 56, 80n, 103
    Duffield on, 59–60
Hynes, William, 31, 71, 72

interdependence
    construction of, 46, 61, 76, 112
    as space to be governed, 42, 78, 97,
    112
International Labour Organisation
    (ILO), the, 51, 63
International Monetary Fund (IMF),
    the, 52, 53, 63
    image/credibility of, 64
    role and influence of, 56, 72
    see also ODA
Ivarsson Holgersson, Carolina, 31

Jackson, Robert H., 92–4, 101, 102

Kant, Immanuel, 105
Kapoor, Ilan, 31, 69, 86, 87, 113n, 114n
Kaul, Inge, 62
Keijzer, Niels, 72, 79
Kindornay, Shannon, 59
Klak, Thomas, 113n
Klekar, Cynthia, 35n

Knack, Stephen, 66
Konstan, David, 27
Kothari, Uma, 42, 63
Kowalski, Robert, 31, 97
Kunkel, Sönke, 39, 63
Kuziemko, Ilyana, 80n

Laidlaw, James, 21–3
Lancaster, Carol, 81n
Larzillière, Pénélope, 59, 61, 80n
Latouche, Serge, 31, 78, 88
Laval, Christian, 10
League of Nations, the, 39–44
    and foreign aid, 41–4
    mandates system of, 40–1
Lemke, Thomas, 32, 36n
León, Rosario, 31
Lessing, Gotthold Ephraim, 98–9
Leviathan, The, 12–13, 109
Lie, Jon Harald Sande, 32, 36n, 53–5,
    79n
Liebersohn, Harry, 10, 11, 15–17, 29, 30
Ludden, David, 61

Macfie, Alec Lawrence, 14
Macrae, Joanna, 70
Magnani, Eliana, 17
Mallard, Grégoire, 18, 30–1
marketisation of aid, 59, 61
    see also privatisation of aid;
    securitisation of development
Marramao, Giacomo, 29
Marshall, Alison, 52, 53
Marshall Plan, the, 42, 43
Maul, Daniel, 64
Mauss, Marcel, 10, 16–22, 30, 31, 35n
    on gift-giving, 17–21
Mawdsley, Emma, 31, 81n
Mawulo-Yevugah, Lord, 36n
McEwan, Cheryl, 113n
McVety, Amanda Kay, 47
Millennium Development Goals, 73, 100,
    101
Miller, Peter, 8
Min, Em Kyung, 14–16
Moore, Gerald, 10

moral duty of material aid
  and benevolence, 103, 106, 114
  and 'development ethics', 103
  in the foreign aid regime, 2, 107–8
  motives/scholars against, 103–4
  motives/scholars in favour of, 104–7
Morgenthau, Hans, 30, 111
Moss, Todd, 66
Mosse, David, 32, 48, 54, 56, 61, 67
Moyo, Dambisa, 66
multilateral aid, *see* multilateral
  organizations
multilateral organizations, 56, 64–6, 68
  image and role of, 64
  relationships with donor states, 65
  see also International Monetary
    Fund; Organisation for Economic
    Co-operation and Development;
    United Nations; World Bank

Natali, Carlo, 27, 28
National Research Council, 39
National Security Council Staff, 78, 79
Naz, Farzana, 85
Nederveen Pieterse, Jan, 64, 87, 88
Nepi, Paolo, 28, 35n
new institutional economics, 57
NGOs, 55, 56, 63, 67, 87
  governmentalization of, 53, 60
  image and role of, 65
  relationships with donors, 65
  credibility of, 65
NIEO Declaration, 64, 100, 102
  criticisms about, 102
Nuijten, Monique, 80n
Nussbaum, Martha C., 80n, 103
Nyerere, Julius, 74–8

O'Neill, Onora, 105–6
ODA (Official Development
  Assistance), 70–3, 81n
  definition and history of, 70–1
  construction of, 72, 73
  and the measurement 'obsession',
    72–3
  what it measures, 71

what it does not measure, 71–2
  see also Organisation for Economic
    Co-operation and Development,
    role of the DAC of
Offer, Avner, 14, 16
Opeskin, Brian R., 102, 104–5, 114n
Organisation for Economic
  Co-operation and Development
  (OECD), the, 63, 70, 72
  role of the DAC of, 71, 73
Osteen, Mark, 11, 28, 84, 109
Owens, Patricia, 100, 112
ownership, technology of, 3, 52–6

participation, technology of, 3, 52–6
Passerin d'Entrèves, Maurizio, 100
Paul, Saint, 25
  on gift-giving, 25–6
Pearson, Lester B., 50–1, 79n
Pearson Report, the, 50–1, 79n
Philpott, Dan, 95, 114n
Pogge, Thomas W., 106, 114n
Point Four Programme, the, 43–7, 76–8
Polanyi, Karl, 35n
policy coherence for development, 79
potlatch, 18–19
Potter, Donald W., 95, 96
Potter, Robert. B., 48
poverty, 49, 51, 54, 56, 76, 84, 87–8, 92
  construction of, 76, 87–8
  as a human right violation, 101, 106
  and inequality of states, 87–8
*Poverty Reduction Strategy Papers
  (PRSPs), the*, 53–6, 57, 64, 79n
privatisation of aid, 59–61
  see also marketisation of aid;
    securitisation of development
Procacci, Giovanna, 88
Pufendorf, Samuel Freiherr von, 89

Qizilbash, Mozaffar, 114n

Raphael, David Daiches, 14
Rapley, John, 49
Ratner, Steven R., 96, 97, 114n
Rawls, John, 106–7, 114n

DOI: 10.1057/9781137505903.0008

Ray, Olivier, 62, 63, 71, 72, 80n
recipient populations
    construction of, 3, 57, 59, 67, 77–8, 88
    fragmentation into selected groups
        of, 2, 4, 83
    see also biopolitics
recipient states
    as failed states, 61, 94, 96
    as indebted states, 3–4, 76–7
    as poor states, 88, 92
    as quasi-states, 92–4
    as untrustworthy states, 67
    see also accountability, of recipients,
        construction of
Red Cross, the, 39
Reilly-King, Fraser, 59
resilience, technology of, 60–1
responsibility to protect, 95, 101, 114n
*Revue du M.A.U.S.S. (Mouvement anti-
    utilitariste dans le sciences sociales)*,
    35n
right to self-determination, 90–1
    Jackson on, 92
    and right to development, 100–1
Riddell, Roger C., 51, 62, 63, 72, 79n,
    80n, 100, 101, 103
Risdale, Frank, 19
Rist, Gilbert, 14, 39–42, 44–7, 49, 74, 75,
    79n, 81n, 86, 113n
risk
    assessment/management, 59, 61
    rationality of, 60
    see also securitisation of
        development
Robinson, William I., 52, 57
Rocha Menocal, Alina, 58
Roland, Kjell, 50, 52, 53, 56, 57, 60, 64,
    70, 79n, 81n
Roodman, David, 70
Rose, Nikolas, 8
Rosenstein-Rodan, Paul Narcyz, 49
Rostow, Walter, 49

Sahlins, Marshall, 30, 100
Satlow, Michael L., 28, 29, 35n
Satz, Debra, 102, 114n

Scott, Simon, 31, 71, 72
securitisation of development, 59–60;
security, and development, 59–60, 62,
    70
Sen, Amartya K., 80n, 88
Seneca, Lucius Anneus, 25
Sengupta, Arjun, 101
Severino, Jean-Michel, 62, 63, 71, 72, 80n
Shenton, Robert W., 62, 68, 87
Shleifer, Andrei, 66
Sidaway, James D., 86, 88, 113n
Silk, John, 31, 60, 65, 114n
Silva, Kelly Cristiane da, 31, 64, 87
Simpson, Gerry, 6, 89–91, 94, 97, 102,
    103, 113n
Singer, Peter, 104–5, 114n
Skøtt Thomsen, Stine, 63, 65
Slim, Hugo, 80n
Smith, Adam, 12, 14
    on gift-giving, 14–15
Soesastro, Hadi, 57
sovereignty
    of donor states, 87
    and foreign aid regime
        governmental rationality, 5, 6, 34,
            54, 83
    Jackson on negative and positive,
        92–3
    and 'legalised hierarchies', 90
    and the principle of sovereign
        equality, 40, 83, 89–92, 113n
    of recipient states, 4, 59, 83
    shifting conceptions of, 95–6
    and substantive inequality, 102–3
    Western conception of, 95, 113n
spatialisation, forms of, 3, 61
Stockholm Initiative, the, 56, 80n
Stokke, Olav, 63–5, 80n, 81n
Strathern, Marilyn, 68
*Structural Adjustment Programmes
    (SAPs), the,* 52–4, 64

Theory of Moral Sentiments, The, 14
Tomasevski, Katarina, 80n
Trujillo, Isabel, 105–6, 114n
Truman, Harry S., 43–4, 46, 76–7, 79n

trust
    in the foreign aid regime, 67–9
    in gift-giving practices, 21, 26, 67
    and mutual accountability, 38, 68
    see also accountability
trusteeship
    development as, 68, 112
    Jackson on, 93
    Helman and Ratner on, 96–7
    United Nations international system
        of, 45
Tschirhart, Christian, 62

United Nations, the, 42–3, 63, 73, 80n,
        96–7
    image/credibility of, 64–5
    role and influence of, 64
United Nations Development
    Programme (UNDP), 56, 58–9, 63
United Nations Global Compact initiative,
        the, 60, 80n
Unger, Corinna R., 39, 44, 63

Van Gastel, Jilles, 80n

Veca, Salvatore, 79n
Veen, A. Maurits van der, 81n
Verhezen, Peter, 24, 29, 36n, 67, 76–7,
        84, 109

Washington consensus, 52, 57, 64
Watt, Patrick, 68
Wealth of Nations, The, 14
Weber, Max, 26
    on the ethics of brotherhood, 27
Wenar, Leif, 106, 114n
Werker, Eric, 80n
White, Howard, 39
Wight, Martin, 89
Williams, David, 72, 95
Woodruff, Martha Kendal, 27–8
World Bank, the, 43, 51, 63
    image/credibility of, 64–5
    role and influence of, 52–3, 56, 72
    see also ODA

Zamagni, Stefano, 10
Zanasi, Margherita, 40–2
Zionkowski, Linda, 35n

DOI: 10.1057/9781137505903.0008

Lightning Source UK Ltd.
Milton Keynes UK
UKOW04n1425170615

253672UK00004B/57/P